More... Memories *from* *my* Kitchen

A Treasure of Favorite Recipes

BARBARA HEIMANN

ISBN: 198205560X
ISBN 13: 9781982055608
Library of Congress Control Number: XXXXX (If applicable)
LCCN Imprint Name: City and State (If applicable)

Cover photo: Elizabeth Stone Feldman
www.SeeingBeyondTheLens.com

Typeset by Jana Singer

MY BEST MEMORY

David
1938-2009

TABLE OF CONTENTS

APPETIZERS

BRUNCH AND EGG DISHES

CAKES, PIES, AND DESSERTS

CANDY AND NUTS

❧

COOKIES

MEAT

MISCELLANEOUS

❧

PASTA, GRAINS, AND RICE

❧

POULTRY

❧

SALAD

❧

SAUCES AND DRESSINGS

❧

SEAFOOD

❧

SOUP

VEGETABLES

PREFACE

I sometimes wonder why people still buy cookbooks. It seems every recipe is on-line. However, if you're like me, I still love to thumb through books and get new ideas or stir my memory back to dishes I used to make. I'm approaching this book as a curator, selecting and sharing some of my choice recipes that I have gathered from friends, family, cookbooks, and restaurateurs. Every recipe has been tested, and when I know the origin, I definitely cite it. Just saying I'm writing a cook-book is a good conversation opener; people want to talk about food and jog their own memories, and though trends in cuisine come and go, I find we still love and rely on our comfort foods. Actually, the publication of this book coincides with my 80th birthday. And had you asked the young me years ago if I would still be interested in cooking and entertaining at this age, I would have said, "No way!", figuring that I would most likely not be active and social at that stage of my life. Well, I'm here to tell you that, fortunately, my friends and I certainly don't feel like the seniors we surely are, and we still enjoy entertaining at home and treating our guests to a special meal, although I no longer feel I have to make every single component. Often I make the main course and supplement with selectively purchased side dishes, or my guests contribute to the meal, rounding out the menu with an appetizer, salad, or a dessert—making entertaining effortless!

I also don't overdo hors d'oeuvres, as then my guests don't have an appetite for dinner. Then again, sometimes I only serve appetizers, and we graze, enjoy the variety, sip a drink, and engage in good conversation.

My children and grandchildren still have their favorites, which I make when they visit. Now, since all my grandchildren are adults, they cook for me and give me recipes. Many of them are outstanding cooks! They are definitely adventurous and discerning eaters!

Cooking really is a passion for me, as it's creative both in the ingredients and the presentation, and it uses almost all the senses. Just hearing a sizzle makes the mouth water!

Luckily, I have many friends who share their recipes with me, and I have attributed their contributions to them. However, I've only used first names for my family, so let me introduce you.

My children: daughter Gloria and Rick Singer; son Bruce and Kathy Heimann; and daughter Stephanie Mallen.

Grandchildren:

Noah and Ilene Singer; Jana Singer and Phoebe Arbogast; Jake Singer; and Marni and Seth Berliner.

Julie and Daniel Arkles, great grandson Hudson David; Lisa and Robin Marriott; and Kevin Mallen.

Alex Heimann, and Cody Heimann.

APPETIZERS

BAKED BRIE

ARTICHOKE SQUARES

2 (6 ounce) jars marinated artichoke hearts

2 medium onions, chopped

1 clove garlic, minced

6 eggs, beaten

½ cup breadcrumbs

½ teaspoon each: salt, pepper, and oregano

Tabasco, to taste (optional)

8 ounces sharp cheddar cheese, shredded

2 tablespoons parsley, chopped fine

TOPPING:

Parmesan, grated

Paprika

Preheat oven to 325 degrees.

Drain marinade into a skillet from one jar of artichokes; drain other jar, and discard that marinade. Chop artichokes and set aside. Sauté onions and garlic in marinade for 5 minutes. Combine eggs, crumbs, seasonings, shredded cheese, onions, and parsley. Add artichokes, and pour into a greased 8×8 inch pan. Bake for 25 minutes. Sprinkle top with grated Parmesan and paprika, and bake 5 minutes longer. Cut into 16 squares.

BAKED BRIE IN PASTRY

This may seem like a "no-brainer" but it's such a lovely presentation and it is always popular at a party—an easy show-stopper!

1 can Pillsbury crescent roll dough

½ cup raspberry jam

1 (12 ounce) round Brie

Preheat oven to 375 degrees.

Roll out dough to an 8×12 inch rectangle. Place Brie in center of dough, and top with the jam; actually any flavor will do. Bring up the dough and twist at the top. Trim the leftover dough, and use the scraps as decoration for the Brie. Place in oven, and bake for 20 to 25 minutes until nicely browned. Slide onto serving platter and scatter walnuts, dried cranberries and apricots around. Wait 5 minutes before slicing into it.

CHEESE STRUDEL

This is a good appetizer to have on hand in the freezer. The recipe makes 4 logs, and 12 pieces can easily be gotten out of each one.

DOUGH:

2½ cups flour

2 sticks butter

1 cup sour cream

FILLING:

3 cups cheddar cheese, shredded

Lawry's salt to taste

Pepper to taste

Paprika to sprinkle on before baking

Combine ingredients for dough in food processor, and pulse until all is combined and forms a ball. Refrigerate for at least 1 hour. When dough is cold, divide into 4 pieces. Roll each piece out into a 6×12 inch rectangle. You may have to add a bit of flour on the board so the dough doesn't stick. Sprinkle Lawry's salt and then pepper on each piece of dough, and cover with ¾ cup cheese. Roll into a log, and slice halfway through into 1-inch servings. Wrap tightly in foil, and freeze. When ready to use, take directly from freezer, and place on baking sheet. Sprinkle log with paprika, and bake at 350 degrees for 30 to 35 minutes.

CHICKEN LIVER PATÉ

This is a riff on Emeril Lagasse's recipe. I served it with crusty French toasts for a French-themed dinner. Also, I was finally able to use the cognac that my sweet father-in-law, Lou Heimann, always brought from Montreal when he visited.

1 pound chicken livers, cleaned

1 cup milk

1 stick butter, divided

1½ cups Vidalia onion, chopped

1 clove garlic, minced

2 tablespoons green peppercorns, drained and divided

2 bay leaves

½ teaspoon dried thyme

½ teaspoon salt

½ teaspoon freshly ground pepper

¼ cup cognac or brandy

½ cup Italian parsley, finely chopped

Cover the livers with milk, and soak for at least 2 hours. Drain well.

In a large pan, melt half the stick of butter, and add the onions, stirring for a few minutes until soft. Add garlic, 1 tablespoon peppercorns, bay leaves, thyme, and salt and pepper. Stir until livers are cooked, but slightly pink on the inside, for about 5 minutes. Add the cognac, and cook until the liquid is evaporated. Cool, and remove bay leaves. Then pulse in the food processor, adding the remaining butter until smooth. Adjust salt and pepper to taste, and fold in the other tablespoon of peppercorns and parsley. Put in a ramekin, and refrigerate until ready to serve. Can easily be done a day ahead.

CHOPPED HERRING

I made chopped herring for "Break Fast". Since I didn't use a recipe, and it turned out so well, I am writing it down while it's still fresh in my memory.

1 (26 ounce) jar pickled herring or herring in wine sauce, drained (Blue Hill Bay from Costco)

2 slices seeded rye bread

2 eggs, hard-boiled

1 apple, peeled, core removed

¼ to ½ large sweet onion

Pinch sugar (optional)

Drain herring fillets, and remove half of the onions in the jar. Pulse rye bread in Cuisinart and set aside. Cut apple, eggs, and onion to same size as herring; then place herring, eggs, apple, and onion into Cuisinart, and pulse until chopped consistency. Add enough breadcrumbs to soak up the juices so the mixture is not too runny. If the herring is too tart, add a bit of sugar to taste.

This can be done several days ahead of when planning to use, and it lasts in fridge for a week.

Serve with rye Melba toast or any cracker of choice.

CLAM FONDUE

I'm thinking of having some friends over to watch the Super Bowl and also thinking that I want to offer this clam fondue as one of the snacks. This has a little "kick" to it - apropos for a football game!

3 tablespoons butter

1 small onion, chopped

½ green pepper, small dice

¼ pound American or cheddar cheese

1 tablespoon milk

4 tablespoons catsup

1 tablespoon Worcestershire

¼ teaspoon cayenne pepper

2 (7 ounce) cans minced clams, drained

2 tablespoons sherry

1 baguette, cubed in mouthful size pieces

Melt butter in pan, and sauté onion and green pepper until just soft. Place onion and pepper in a microwave safe bowl, and add rest of the ingredients except clams and sherry. Microwave cheese mixture one minute at a time until cheese is melted. And then add clams and sherry. Serve in a fondue pot or over a small flame. Have some skewered crusty bread cubes on hand for dipping.

EGG SALAD WITH THOUSAND ISLAND DRESSING

Ellen Gersh elevates this humble appetizer to party status!

Serves 8–10

Thousand Island Dressing:

¼ cup mayonnaise, can be light

2 tablespoons catsup

2 tablespoons sweet pickle relish, patted dry

Mix all together.

EGG SALAD:

10 eggs, hard-boiled

¼ cup scallions, finely minced

⅓ cup mayonnaise, can be light

Salt and pepper to taste

Mash egg ingredients together, and place in plastic wrap-lined bowl. When ready to serve, turn out on plate and "ice" with the dressing. Serve with crackers.

GOUGÈRE WITH GREEN ONION

I usually make the gougères and freeze them before baking.
Then whenever I need a quick, impressive appetizer—voilà!

1 cup water

¾ stick (6 tablespoons) unsalted butter

1 teaspoon kosher salt

2 dashes white pepper

1 cup plus 2 tablespoons flour

4 extra-large eggs

1½ cups extra sharp white cheddar cheese

⅔ cup minced green onion

Bring water, butter, and salt to a boil. Remove from heat, and put in flour all at once. Stir over medium heat until dough becomes shiny and pulls away from sides of pan, at least 2 minutes. Put in mixer with paddle; add eggs, 1 at a time, and mix each one until thoroughly incorporated. Finally, add cheese and onion. Drop from a soup spoon onto parchment paper to form 1½-inch ovals. Can freeze at this stage. Bake at 375 degrees for 30 minutes if at room temperature and for 35 minutes if frozen.

HOT ARTICHOKE SPREAD

This is a bit different from most of the others that only use mayo and Parmesan. You might want to cut the recipe in half unless you have about 12 people having appetizers!

2 (10 ounce) packages frozen artichokes, thawed

2 (8 ounce) packages cream cheese

⅔ cup mayonnaise, Hellman's light

1⅓ cups sour cream, reduced fat

2 cups grated Parmesan

Pinch of prepared garlic puree

Pinch of dill

Pinch of paprika

Cut each artichoke heart in half lengthwise.

Combine them in a bowl with the cream cheese, mayonnaise, sour cream, Parmesan, garlic (just a bit, don't overpower artichokes), and dill.

Spoon into an oven-proof serving bowl or rectangular dish.

Sprinkle top with paprika, and bake at 350 degrees for 30 minutes.

Serve with crackers.

JARLSBERG TOASTS

This is another of Ellen Gersh's recipes. Very tasty!

1 Vidalia onion, chopped

Butter for sautéing onion

8 ounces Jarlsberg cheese grated, can be light

½ cup mayonnaise, can be light

Preheat oven to 375 degrees.

Gently sauté onions in a bit of butter just until wilted and lightly golden. Mix onion with Jarlsberg, and add enough mayonnaise just to bind. Spread on French bread toasts, and bake until puffed and caramel colored.

MEXICAN CORN DIP, BAKED

Ginny Foreman served this with some corn chips as a bite before going out to dinner.

1 (15–16 ounce) can of Mexican corn

6 ounces Swiss cheese, shredded

1 (15 ounce) can black beans, drained

1 cup mayonnaise, can use light mayo

Preheat oven to 350 degrees.

Lightly spray 8-inch oven-proof dish with oil. Stir all ingredients together, and place in dish.

Bake for 40 minutes or until lightly browned and bubbly.

*The mixture can be placed in several small gratin dishes and baked. Just watch the time in oven, as it will be shorter.

Blot top with paper towel if too greasy. Serve with corn chips or tortilla chips. This recipe can easily be doubled.

MIDDLE EASTERN PITA SPREADS

Lisa, Robin, and I were at the Ritz Poolside Café for lunch, and we ordered an appetizer of 3 mezzes, a perfect dish to share with some warmed pita. Luckily for us, they were kind enough to share the recipes for this book. I made some very slight adjustments.

❧

CURRIED LENTIL HUMMUS

½ cup yellow lentils (can substitute with any lentil)

4 leaves curry (can buy on Amazon)

2 teaspoons curry powder

1 teaspoon turmeric, ground

1 jalapeño, cut in half, seeded

2 teaspoons kosher salt

¾ cup extra virgin olive oil

1 (15 ounce) can chickpeas, drained

½ cup lemon juice from 2 large lemons

2 tablespoons tahini paste

1 tablespoon cumin, ground

½ teaspoon cayenne pepper

6 cloves garlic, roasted and then minced

1 teaspoon paprika

Roast garlic cloves with a bit of oil added, wrapped in aluminum foil, in a 350-degree oven for 12 to 15 minutes. Cool, and mince. Place lentils in saucepan with 1½ cups water. Add curry leaves, curry powder, turmeric, and jalapeño, and bring to a boil; then cover, and simmer for 20 minutes. Cool, and remove curry leaves and jalapeño.

Mix the cumin, cayenne, garlic, salt, lemon juice, and tahini, and make slurry.

In the food processor, blend chickpeas, lentils, and slurry; add olive oil ¼ cup at a time, and pulse after each addition. Process until smooth. Freezes well.

MUHAMMARA

Yields 1 quart

4 ounces walnuts

3 ounces panko breadcrumbs

4 cloves garlic, peeled

1 tablespoon molasses

1 tablespoon cumin

1 teaspoon kosher salt

¼ cup olive oil

6 red bell peppers

Preheat oven to 450 degrees.

Roast peppers in hot oven for 20 to 25 minutes, turning twice, until slightly charred and soft.

Immediately place peppers in a bowl, and cover tightly with aluminum foil. Let sit until cool enough to handle. Then peel the peppers, and remove seeds—set aside.

Pulse the peppers in a food processor with the remaining ingredients while drizzling with olive oil.

Season to taste. This freezes well, just place some plastic wrap directly over preparation before putting on lid to container.

TRADITIONAL HUMMUS

Yields 1 quart

20 ounces cooked chickpeas or 1½ (15 ounce) cans, rinsed and drained)
½ cup roasted garlic
4 tablespoons tahini paste
3 tablespoons olive oil
3 tablespoons lemon juice
1 teaspoon ginger, ground
1 teaspoon coriander, ground
2 teaspoons paprika
1 tablespoon cumin

1 tablespoon salt

1 teaspoon cayenne pepper

1 teaspoon garlic powder

Roast garlic in olive oil until golden brown; drain excess oil, and reserve. Process chickpeas and garlic until smooth in food processor. Combine all remaining ingredients; process until smooth. Adjust seasoning to taste.

PEA AND ARTICHOKE SPREAD

2 cups frozen peas, thawed

½ cup drained marinated artichoke hearts, reserve oil

1 teaspoon reserved artichoke oil

¼ cup feta cheese, crumbled

3 tablespoons mint, chopped

3 tablespoons lemon juice

1 tablespoon olive oil or tahini

1 teaspoon garlic, minced

Salt and pepper to taste

Process all ingredients until chunky, and then season with salt and pepper. Serve with baked pita chips.

ROASTED RED PEPPER PESTO

At Saquella, one of our favorite places for brunch, Gloria and Rick shared a Mediterranean cheese plate, which featured this pesto. After tasting it, I came up with this rendition.

4 ounces asiago cheese

1 clove garlic

1 teaspoon fresh basil

1 (12 ounce) jar fire-roasted red peppers, drained; or 1½ large peppers, roasted, seeded, and peeled

½ (8 ½ ounce) jar sun-dried tomatoes packed in olive oil

½ teaspoon salt

Several grinds black pepper

2 tablespoons pignoli nuts, toasted

Place asiago in food processor with garlic and basil, and pulse until cheese is coarsely grated. Add peppers, tomatoes, and salt, and pulse until thick spreading consistency. Add pignoli nuts, and whir until all is blended, just a few seconds. Taste, and add more salt and pepper if needed. Serve with toasted baguette slices.

*I like to use the Dorot frozen garlic and basil for this preparation. Use 1 cube of the garlic and 1 cube of the basil. Dorot frozen herbs can be found in the frozen foods department of many grocery stores.

SHRIMP, NOT COCKTAIL

This is an old favorite, very easy to make, and a good buffet dish for cocktail hour.

3 pounds cooked shrimp, tail off, cut in half from head to tail

2 Vidalia onions, thinly sliced

1 pint Miracle Whip, can use light

⅓ cup lemon juice

1–2 tablespoons sugar (optional)

4 tablespoons capers, drained (optional)

In a large bowl, mix Miracle Whip, lemon juice, and sugar, if you like a little sweetness. And then place shrimp and onions into the bowl, and mix through. Cover and chill for 24 hours. When ready to serve, spoon the shrimp from the mixing bowl into a serving dish with some small plates and cocktail forks alongside.

SILJANS CRISPY CUP FILLINGS

I like to keep a box of these Siljan cups on hand, and then just let my imagination go. Sandy Roth filled them with finely diced ingredients for a BLT mixed with light mayo. I took the Brie with jam and pistachios to a condo party, and though I made a lot, there wasn't one left! You also could use miniature filo cups.

Always place the cheese in the bottom of the cup, and then add other ingredients.

Cream cheese, smoked salmon, capers, and dill sprig. Serve this cold.

Bake the following at 375 degrees for 7–10 minutes until melted and bubbling. Add nuts after baking.

- a. Brie with pear and walnuts.
- b. Brie with jam of choice. I like apricot or fig with crushed pistachios on top.
- c. Gruyère cheese melted in microwave, topped with cherry tomato.

❧

SMOKED FISH PATÉ

Legal Seafood is a well-known Boston restaurant, and this is one of their most popular appetizers.

1 pound smoked fish fillets

8 ounces cream cheese

¼ cup butter

2 tablespoons cognac

¼ cup minced onion

½ teaspoon Worcestershire sauce

2 tablespoons fresh lemon juice

Salt and pepper to taste

Walnuts, toasted and finely chopped (optional)

In a food processor, puree the fish, cream cheese, butter, and cognac. Then add the onion, Worcestershire, and lemon juice. Pulse until just combined. Season with salt and pepper to taste. Pack into a ramekin and sprinkle with nuts, if desired. Chill. Serve with crackers or toasts.

SMOKED SALMON ROULADE

I take cooking classes from the chefs at Ritz Carlton, and I usually come away with a clever technique. This recipe is easy, great to have on hand in the freezer, and it makes a lovely presentation. I make this even if I don't have a pound of smoked salmon, especially if I've used the salmon with bagels and have some left over.

1 pound smoked salmon

1 container of Boursin cheese, room temperature

Lay out a piece of plastic wrap, about 18 inches long, length facing you. Place slices of smoked salmon, overlapping to form a rectangle about 10×8 inches. When you are satisfied with the base, spread soft Boursin over the salmon.

Then starting from the bottom, and using the plastic wrap, roll the salmon into a log form, coaxing it along with the plastic wrap. And then encase the log in the plastic wrap and tie one end. Carefully form the log into a uniform shape and tie off the open end. The log should be about 2 inches in diameter. Place in freezer, and when ready to use, slice off as many ¼-inch pieces as you need. Place on a round cracker, and serve.

BRUNCH AND EGG DISHES

APRICOT BREAD PUDDING

I met Nancy Sklar at Bridge Camp in the Berkshires. At breakfast one morning, we started talking about recipes, and I asked for a few of her best. This is one of them.

Serves 8–10

1 cup raisins

¼ cup boiling water

3 cups milk

1 cup light cream

5 extra-large eggs, room temperature

1 cup sugar

¼ teaspoon salt

3 tablespoons vanilla

½ teaspoon almond extract

10 slices firm white bread, crusts removed, cut into cubes

Butter, unsalted, as needed—up to ½ cup

1 (12 ounce) jar apricot preserves

1 tablespoon Grand Marnier (optional)

Preheat oven to 375 degrees.

Soak raisins in boiling water for 5 minutes; drain and set aside. Scald milk and cream in a saucepan over medium heat just until bubbles form around the edge. Remove from heat to cool.

In a large bowl, whisk the eggs and sugar; then gradually add the warm milk, salt, vanilla, and almond extract, while continuing to whisk the mixture. Generously butter a 3-quart baking dish, and place the bread cubes in the dish. Sprinkle the bread with raisins, and then slowly pour the milk mixture over. Dot the top with the butter.

Meanwhile, in a small saucepan, heat the apricot preserves over low heat until spreading consistency. Add the Grand Marnier if using, and spoon the apricot preserves over the top of the bread mixture. Bake for 45 minutes until firm and golden brown. Serve warm or at room temperature. If you feel like adding a few calories, some vanilla ice cream will do the trick!

AVOCADO TOAST FOR TWO

Kevin has become a good cook since spending 5 years in Australia.
We're happy to have him home!

4 slices good quality bread, toasted

1 large avocado

Cherry tomatoes, quartered

Feta

Mint, fresh or dried

Lemon juice

Dukkah (Egyptian spice blend available on Amazon)

Radishes, thinly sliced

Cut avocado in half, and scoop out the flesh. Mash with some lemon juice to prevent discoloring. Add the tomatoes, feta, and mint in proportions to your liking. Spread avocado onto the toasted bread, and sprinkle with dukkah. Top with the radishes, and devour immediately!

AVO TOAST WITH EGGS

1 avocado mashed with 1 tablespoon lemon juice and a pinch salt

4 eggs

4 slices toast

½ cup fresh spinach_(optional)

¼ cup cucumbers, sliced thinly

6 ounces smoked salmon

Cook eggs any way you like, even hard-boiled. Spread avocado mixture on each slice of toast and layer spinach, salmon, and top with eggs. Season with salt and pepper.

BLINTZ BRUNCH BITES

Sandy Roth made these for brunch when she and Ronnie co-hosted with the Myers and Warshauers the morning after my 80th birthday party.

2 (8 ounce) packages cream cheese, softened

½ cup sugar

2 egg yolks

2 (16 ounce) loaves white bread, thinly sliced, crusts removed

2 sticks (1 cup) butter, melted

Cinnamon and sugar mixture

Preheat oven to 400 degrees.

In mixing bowl, combine cream cheese, sugar, and egg yolks. Beat until smooth.

Between 2 sheets of waxed paper, flatten each bread slice with a rolling pin.

Spread bread with cream cheese mixture. Roll up jellyroll fashion. Brush with melted butter. Sprinkle cinnamon/sugar over.

Bake seam side down on ungreased cookie sheet until lightly browned.

Can be frozen, then baked.

Bake at 400 degrees 8–10 minutes, or 10–15 minutes, if frozen.

BLINTZ SOUFFLÉ

This is such an easy recipe, you'll be embarrassed by all the raves it gets!

Serves 12

12 frozen cheese blintzes or fruit blintzes

1½ teaspoons vanilla

1 stick butter, melted

¼ cup plus 2 tablespoons orange juice

¼ cup plus two tablespoons sugar

9 eggs

3 cups sour cream

Preheat oven to 350 degrees.

Spray or butter a 4-quart Pyrex. Line dish with the blintzes.

Combine all other ingredients in blender or mixer until light and frothy. Pour over blintzes. Bake 50 to 60 minutes until lightly browned and puffed. If using the cheese blintzes, serve with the following berry sauce.

STRAZZBERRY SAUCE

1 quart strawberries

1 tablespoon sugar

1 (10 ounce) package frozen raspberries, thawed

1 tablespoon orange liquor

Wash and drain strawberries. Slice and sprinkle with sugar. In processor, puree raspberries with orange liquor. Two hours before serving, ladle sauce over strawberries. Excellent over blintz soufflé.

EGG-WHITE FRITTATA WITH SMOKED SALMON

8 large egg whites

½ cup half and half

6 ounces smoked salmon, medium chop

Grated zest of 1 lemon

½ teaspoon salt

Black pepper

2 tablespoons vegetable oil

2 cups arugula, packed fully

1 clove garlic, minced

Preheat oven to 350 degrees.

Whisk egg whites until fluffy; add half and half, salmon, lemon zest, and seasonings. Heat oil over medium heat in oven-proof skillet. Add arugula and garlic, and cook until just wilted. Pour in egg mixture. Cook without stirring for 4 minutes. Place skillet on center rack in oven, and bake for 10 minutes until eggs are set. Slide onto a platter, and cut into wedges. Can be served at room temperature.

FRENCH TOAST WITH PEARS AND RASPBERRIES

I'm always looking for recipes that can be done the day before, especially when it comes to brunch. I saw this in Martha Stewart's Living Magazine and decided to make it for Lisa and Robin's arrival after a red-eye flight from Denver. The condo had a warm, welcoming deliciousness when they got in. This is now my favorite brunch recipe!

Serves 8–10

1 loaf challah, sliced ¾-inch thick

3 Bosc pears, peeled and thinly sliced

1½ to 2 cups raspberries

½ cup sugar

1 teaspoon cinnamon

1 teaspoon salt

8 large eggs

2 cups whole milk (I use 2%)

2 teaspoons vanilla

Cinnamon/sugar for sprinkling on top

Butter a 3-quart baking dish, and arrange the challah, pears, and raspberries evenly in overlapping layers.

In a large bowl, mix the sugar, cinnamon, and salt. Add the eggs, milk, and vanilla and whisk vigorously to combine. Pour the egg mixture over the challah, pressing ingredients down to make sure they are submerged. At this point, let stand at room temperature before baking, or place in fridge overnight. Just before baking, sprinkle cinnamon/sugar mixture over top.

Bake at 350 degrees for 55 to 65 minutes.

GARDEN VEGGIE QUICHE (NO CRUST)

Serves 10

1¾ cups egg whites

3 extra-large eggs

6 ounces shredded lo-fat cheddar, divided

6 ounces shredded lo-fat Monterey Jack, divided

½ cup lo-fat milk

⅓ cup flour

1 teaspoon baking powder

½ teaspoon salt

16 ounces reduced fat cottage cheese

1 leek, white only, sliced thin

1 red or green pepper, chopped

12 ounces pre-sliced mushrooms

2 zucchini, sliced

2 cups Simply Potatoes with onions

½ cup chopped parsley

2 tomatoes, thinly sliced, optional

Preheat oven to 400 degrees.

Sauté leek, pepper, and mushrooms for about 5 minutes until wilted. Add zucchini. Set aside. This can be done the day prior to baking the quiche. Refrigerate if completing the recipe the next day. When ready to prepare, beat all eggs together until fluffy. Add milk, flour, baking powder, and salt and beat well. Add cottage cheese and half of each of the cheeses. Add sautéed veggies and parsley to eggs. Place in greased 3-quart casserole. Top with remaining cheese and arrange tomato slices, if using, over top. Bake for 15 minutes. Reduce heat to 350 degrees, and bake for 35 minutes more until set and puffed.

Note: Be creative. Add turkey sausage or different vegetables to this quiche.

ILENE'S BREAKFAST CASSEROLE

My grandson Noah's wife, Ilene, made this casserole when I was visiting them in New York. She got it from her cousin Sarah, and I'm very happy to pass this one along.

8 ounces sharp cheddar cheese, grated

16 ounces cottage cheese

6 eggs, beaten

¼ cup melted butter

1 cup milk

1 cup pancake mix (Aunt Jemimah or similar)

½–1 cup sliced mushrooms (optional)

Several shakes Trader Joe's 21 Seasoning Salute or other herb seasoning of your choice or salt and pepper

3 ounces French's fried onions

Preheat oven to 350 degrees.

Combine all ingredients except French's fried onions. Pour into greased 9×13 inch baking dish or 2-quart round casserole dish. Sprinkle French's onions on top. Bake 35–40 minutes. Onions should be brown and crispy.

This is Ilene's response to my question asking if this can be prepared ahead: "You definitely can. I recommend combining everything in a bowl (except for the onions) to refrigerate overnight and giving it a big stir in the morning before pouring into the cooking dish as it tends to separate overnight."

JARLSBERG EGG BAKE

I made this for my brunch group that meets once a month. Perfect alongside lox and bagels!

Serves 8–10

14 eggs

⅔ cup sour cream

¼ cup sherry

¾ teaspoon salt

4 cups shredded Swiss cheese, Jarlsberg preferred

⅓ cup chopped pimento

Preheat oven to 350 degrees.

In mixer, beat eggs until fluffy, and then add sour cream, sherry, and salt, and beat on low until well combined. Fold in cheese and pimento by hand. Pour into greased 3-quart casserole. Bake for 30–40 minutes until set.

NOODLE KUGEL

I was at Gloria's for the high holidays, looking through her menus from past years, and came upon this recipe she got from Laura Werner. I like this because it uses only 8 ounces of noodles, is quite creamy, and just sweet enough!

½ pound wide noodles

2 eggs

½ pint sour cream

½ pound cottage cheese

½ stick melted butter

½ cup sugar

½ teaspoon salt

1 teaspoon vanilla

1 (8 ounce) can crushed pineapple, drained well

1 (8 ounce) can peaches, drained

Cook noodles; butter 3-quart casserole.

Mix rest of ingredients into the noodles.

Sprinkle cinnamon on top. Bake for 1 hour at 350 degrees.

POPOVERS BOBBIE'S WAY

As soon as these "pop" out of the oven, serve them! These are a favorite of Bobbie and Jack Myers. Change it up by adding 2 tablespoons sugar to this recipe and you'll have a Dutch Baby fluffy pancake.

1 stick salted butter

6 eggs

1½ cups milk

1½ cups flour

Sprinkle cinnamon

Preheat oven to 400 degrees.

Place butter in 9×13 inch pan and set in oven to melt while mixing batter.

Beat eggs in a blender for 1 minute, add milk and flour and continue to blend for 30 seconds. Slowly pour the batter into the pan with melted butter, and sprinkle some cinnamon over. Bake at 400 degrees until puffy and brown—25 to 30 minutes. Do not open oven while baking! Serve immediately with powdered sugar, fruit, jam, or syrup on the side.

RICOTTA FRITTATA

The name of this dish sounds like it could be a new dance craze, and actually eating this frittata makes you want to sing. If you have a large iron skillet, use it to cook this frittata. Anita Shapiro made this for our bridge lunch and served it with some fresh berries and lemon cookies. Just perfect!

Serves 6

1½ cups mushrooms, sliced

2 tablespoons butter

12 eggs

1½ teaspoons salt

½ cup plus 2 tablespoons cream or milk

1½ cups ricotta cheese

½ cup sharp cheddar cheese, grated

1½ cups frozen peas

1 cup cherry tomatoes, halved

¼ cup fresh herbs of your choice, finely chopped

¼ cup Parmesan cheese, grated

Preheat oven to 400 degrees.

In the oven-proof skillet you will be using, sauté the mushrooms in the butter for about 5 minutes until browned. In the meantime, whisk the eggs and salt together, and add the cream, cheddar, and ricotta. Stir just to combine, and add the frozen peas, tomatoes, mushrooms, and herbs. Return this mixture to the skillet. Dust the Parmesan over the frittata, and bake for 35 to 40 minutes until set.

RICOTTA SPINACH PIE

I decided to try to get my brunch group together since we hadn't been able to meet at all during the high season in Naples. What with one thing and another, people moving, so much company, etc., we just couldn't pull one Sunday a month out of the calendar! It turned out Easter Sunday worked for us, but since it was still Passover, I wanted a menu that would follow the traditional dietary rules. This pie just fit the bill!

Serves 8

2 tablespoons olive oil

1 onion, large and thinly sliced

16 ounces fresh spinach, pre-washed, sliced into ribbons

1 (16 ounce) container ricotta cheese

5 eggs

¼ cup egg whites

6 ounces feta cheese, crumbled

1 tablespoon oregano, dried

1 tablespoon za'atar

1 teaspoon salt

Pepper to taste

Pine nuts, optional

Preheat oven to 350 degrees.

Heat oil in large frying pan, and add onions. Reduce heat to medium, and cook until just beginning to get a bit of color, about 8 to 10 minutes. Add the spinach in batches; it wilts quickly, and then you can add more. Continue to sauté until spinach is just wilted (This mixture can be refrigerated, even overnight, until ready to put pie together).

In a bowl, mix the ricotta and eggs together, and then add the feta and seasonings. Finally add the spinach mixture, being careful not to add the juice that has accumulated in the pan.

Pour this mixture into a lightly greased 12-inch round shallow baking dish or a 9×13. Sprinkle a handful of pine nuts over the top, pressing them lightly into the mixture. Bake at 350 degrees for 50–60 minutes, until center is firm and slightly puffed.

RICOTTA ON TOAST

This is another one of Kevin's go-to's. In his words, he adorns the toast with a Parmesan crisp on top to "pizazz it".

Serves 4–6

Good-quality bread, toasted

1½ cups peas, defrosted

¾ cup ricotta cheese

2 tablespoons mint leaves

1 tablespoon lemon zest

Lemon juice to taste

Olive oil as needed

*Parmesan crisps (These can be bought, or easily made).

This can be expanded for any number of people. Brush oil on bread and toast in oven. Depending on size of bread, use 4 to 6 slices for this amount of spread. Process or mash the peas, ricotta, lemon, and mint together to make a textured spread. Add a bit of olive oil if too dry. Stand Parmesan crisps on top, and eat up!

*To make Parmesan crisps, pour individual heaping tablespoons of Parmesan onto parchment- lined baking sheet and lightly pat down, spacing the spoonfuls ½ an inch apart. Bake for 3 to 5 minutes or until golden and crisp.

SHAKSHUKA

When Lisa returned from a birthright trip to Israel, she called and asked me how to make shakshuka. As I had never had it in Israel, she described the dish to me. In the meantime, I was visiting Jana and Phoebe in Chicago, and Jana made this for breakfast, being sure to write down everything as she prepared the dish. Now, it seems shakshuka is on many breakfast menus in the U.S. This recipe is for 4 to 6, but just adjust amounts for sauce, and add as many eggs as needed. Also adjust skillet size! In a pinch, omit the tomatoes and use a marinara sauce as the base for the vegetables. Use whatever veggies you like—go crazy!

2 tablespoons olive oil

1 yellow onion

2–3 cloves garlic, minced

2½ teaspoons cumin

2½ teaspoons coriander

2 bell peppers, any color, diced

1 jalapeño, very small dice

½ eggplant, diced

1 teaspoon salt

1 teaspoon pepper

3 tomatoes, chopped

1 (6 ounce) can tomato paste

¼ teaspoon caraway seeds, ground

2 teaspoons apple cider vinegar or lemon juice

¼ teaspoon sugar

½ cup Italian parsley, chopped

Harissa paste, hot pepper sauce, or red pepper flakes to taste (optional)

Eggs, at least 1 per person

¼ cup feta cheese

Garnishes: cilantro, chives, Greek yogurt, mint, and harissa

Cover bottom of cast iron pan or any deep pan with the olive oil. Add onion, garlic, cumin, and coriander. Stir well, and cook over medium heat for 5 minutes or until onions begin to soften.

Add bell peppers, jalapeño, and eggplant. Season with the salt and pepper. Continue cooking until vegetables are very soft, 7–10 minutes.

Reduce heat to medium low, and add tomatoes, tomato paste, and caraway seeds. Continue to cook another 5 minutes. Add vinegar and sugar and stir. Adjust seasonings and stir in parsley.

Using a large spoon create depressions in the vegetable mixture for each egg. Be careful not to go as deep as bottom of pan. Crack 1 egg into each depression to nestle in the mixture. Sprinkle feta cheese over the veggies. Cover pan, and cook for 8–10 minutes until eggs are just set.

Serve with toasted baguette and the garnishes alongside.

SPINACH EGG BAKE

Gloria made this for my 75th birthday brunch. Time flies...

1 onion, sliced, and sautéed

1 (12 ounce) box mushrooms, sliced, and sautéed

Place these ingredients in bottom of a 9×13- inch oven-proof dish.

8 extra-large eggs

⅓ cup egg whites

2 (10 ounce) boxes frozen chopped spinach, thawed, and drained well

2 (6 ounce) containers plain yogurt (I use Greek Chobani plain)

8 ounces shredded cheese, can use a mix of cheddar and mozzarella or whatever you have on hand (feta is good too)

Salt and pepper to taste

Small handful of chopped fresh parsley or dill

Baby tomatoes, halved—just enough to lightly cover egg mixture

Za'atar

Whisk eggs and egg whites together, and add rest of the ingredients.

Blend well, then spread on top of onions and mushrooms.

Top with some sliced baby tomatoes, and then spread over a bit more cheese, and sprinkle some za'atar (Middle Eastern seasoning blend) on top.

Bake at 350 degrees for approximately 1 hour until set and bubbly. These can be pre-baked for about 45 minutes, and then refrigerated for up to a day before returning to the oven to finish the baking. If you do this, bring to room temperature before placing in the oven.

Use any vegetables you like; just keep proportion of eggs to yogurt.

BARBARA HEIMANN

SPINACH, MUSHROOM, AND CHEESE STRATA

Louise Warshauer made this for our brunch group—delicious!

Serves 8–10

4 tablespoons extra-virgin olive oil, plus more for greasing the dish

6–8 cups rustic Italian bread, crust removed, cut into 1-inch cubes

Kosher salt and freshly ground black pepper

10 ounces cremini mushrooms, sliced (about 4 cups)

2 cloves garlic, minced

1 teaspoon fresh thyme leaves, roughly chopped

5 ounces fresh baby spinach (about 5 cups)

4 ounces Gruyère, shredded on the large holes of a box grater (about 1½ cups)

⅓ cup grated Parmesan

8 large eggs

2½ cups half-and-half

Grease a 9×13- inch (3-quart) casserole dish with oil.

Toss the bread cubes with 2 tablespoons of the oil, ¼ teaspoon salt, and a few grinds of pepper in a large bowl. Bake at 350 degrees for 20–30 minutes. Heat the remaining 2 tablespoons oil over medium-high heat until it starts to shimmer. Add the mushrooms in one layer (resist the urge to stir right away), and cook until they start to brown, about 3 minutes; stir and continue to brown for 2 minutes more. Add the garlic, thyme, ¼ teaspoon salt, and some pepper; stir continuously for 1 minute, and then fold in the spinach and another ¼ teaspoon salt. Continue to cook, stirring often, until the spinach is wilted, 1–2 minutes.

Place half the bread cubes in the prepared casserole dish, and sprinkle them with half of each of the Gruyère and Parmesan. Add the mushroom-spinach mixture in an even layer. Top with the remaining bread cubes, Gruyère, and Parmesan.

In a large bowl, whisk together the eggs, half-and-half, ½ teaspoon salt, and several grinds of pepper. Pour the egg mixture into the casserole dish. Cover with plastic wrap, and refrigerate for at least 6 hours up to overnight. Remove the casserole from the refrigerator 30 minutes before baking.

Preheat the oven to 350 degrees. Bake the casserole until the custard is set and the top is golden brown, 50–55 minutes. Cool for at least 15 minutes before serving warm or at room temperature.

SPINACH AND THREE-CHEESE KUGEL

6–8 servings

8 ounces wide egg noodles

3 tablespoons unsalted butter

¼ cup onion, finely chopped

2 tablespoons parsley, chopped

1 (10 ounce) package frozen chopped spinach

¾ cup sour cream

1 cup small curd cottage cheese

2 eggs, beaten

¼ cup Parmesan cheese, grated

½ cup Swiss cheese, shredded

1 teaspoon salt

½ teaspoon white pepper

½ teaspoon thyme

Dash of nutmeg

Preheat oven to 350 degrees.

Cook and drain noodles. Toss with 2 tablespoons butter. Sauté onion and parsley for 5 minutes in remaining tablespoon butter.

Fold into the noodles.

Defrost and thoroughly drain the spinach. Fold it into the noodles with the sour cream, cottage cheese, eggs, Parmesan cheese, Swiss cheese, and seasonings. Pour into greased 2-quart baking dish. Cover with aluminum foil, and bake for 45 minutes. Remove the foil, and cook for 15 minutes longer.

STEPHANIE'S FRITTATA

When I was in Denver and staying with Stephanie, she made this casserole for breakfast. We ate it over the next few days—nice to have for a ready-made breakfast, easily rewarmed in the microwave. When I returned to Naples, I had some friends over for brunch and served this as the center-piece dish with small portions of baked salmon; a cucumber in tzatziki salad; fresh fruit salad—peaches, nectarines, and blueberries; and some mini cinnamon walnut scones.

8 ounces mushrooms

½ (6 ounce) bag spinach

6 eggs

⅓ cup milk

4 ounces cheddar, grated

5 thin slices Dave's Good Seed Bread, cut into 1-inch pieces

1 ½ tablespoons olive oil

Paprika

1 cup baby tomatoes, halved

Preheat oven to 400 degrees.

Sauté mushrooms in a bit of olive oil. When they have released their juices and are just about dry, add the spinach, and cook until just wilted.

In a bowl, beat 6 eggs with the milk, and then add the sautéed veggies to the eggs. Mix in the cheese, add the bread to this, and set aside.

Place a 2-quart casserole with 1½ tablespoons olive oil in the oven for 5 minutes until the oil is very hot. Remove from oven, and pour in the egg mixture. Sprinkle paprika over the top, and then throw the tomatoes on top of that.

Bake at 400 degrees for ½ hour or until eggs are set.

SWEET NOODLE KUGEL WITH PEACHES

Pauline Hendel brought this ambrosial kugel to "Break Fast".

4 or 5 peaches or apples, peeled and sliced

16 ounces broad noodles

4 quarts water

2 teaspoons salt

8 ounces (2 sticks) butter (includes amount for greasing pan)

3 tablespoons cinnamon/sugar mixture

1 (16 ounce) jar apricot preserves

4 eggs, well beaten

¾ cup white raisins

Preheat oven to 325 degrees.

*Blanch peaches and then peel, remove pits, and slice them.

Boil noodles in water mixed with salt. When noodles are al dente, drain, and melt the butter in the hot noodles. Then mix in the cinnamon/sugar mixture, apricot preserves, eggs, and finally the fruit and raisins.

Butter 9×13 inch baking dish and fill with noodle mixture. Bake for 1½ hours.

Cover with foil if top gets too brown.

To blanch peaches:

Make an X at the base of each peach.

Submerge peaches in boiling water. Boil for 1 minute.

Meanwhile prepare ice bath.

Remove peaches with slotted spoon, and place into ice bath. Let cool for a minute or two, and drain.

Using a paring knife, get under the skin at the base, and slip the skin off.

ZUCCHINI AND CORN FRITTERS WITH CHUTNEY

Julie and Daniel had the Colorado contingent over for brunch on Mother's Day, and what a great meal—very well prepared! Julie makes everything from scratch. In addition to delicious strata, she made these fritters, which we were eating hot out of the pan. She got the recipe from the Food Network Kitchen.

2 medium zucchini, coarsely grated

½ teaspoon salt

1 tablespoon unsalted butter

½ small onion, finely chopped

1 clove garlic, minced

2 ears corn, kernels removed

½ cup yellow cornmeal

½ cup flour

¼ teaspoon baking soda

¾ teaspoon salt

Freshly ground pepper

¾ cup buttermilk

1 large egg

Vegetable oil, for frying

Toss the zucchini with the salt, and let sit in bowl for 10 minutes. Then squeeze the zucchini dry—a towel can be used for this. Heat butter, and cook onion and garlic about 4 minutes to soften. Add corn, and cook just until crisp tender—a few minutes. Set aside.

Mix the dry ingredients together, and add to the wet ingredients. Stir until just combined.

Heat about ⅛ inch of oil in skillet. Working in batches, scoop ¼ cupful of the batter into the oil; flatten a bit with the back of a spoon. Cook about 3 minutes per side until golden brown. Drain on paper towels; sprinkle with salt. These can be made 2 hours ahead and reheated on a rack in a 375 degree oven. Serve with chutney.

JULIE'S CHUTNEY (IN HER OWN WORDS)

"There's not really a recipe for the chutney, but here is what I put in it (ish)."

½ onion

3 cloves garlic

3 whole tomatoes (seeds and pulp discarded), chopped

1 tablespoon brown sugar

1 tablespoon apple cider vinegar

Small handful raisins

Pinch of cloves

Grated nutmeg, probably about ½–1 teaspoon

1 teaspoon paprika

1 teaspoon red pepper flakes

Salt and pepper to taste

"I just heated up about a tablespoon of olive oil and a tablespoon of butter in a pan. Sautéed the onions and garlic until softened; added the tomatoes along with the rest of the ingredients, and then simmered for 20 minutes covered."

CAKES, PIES, AND DESSERTS

PEACH PIE

BLUEBERRY APPLE CRISP

This is one of Arlene Subin's favorite recipes. Look at the ingredients—just makes you want to try it. Arlene likes to serve the crisp with some vanilla ice cream on the side.

1 cup flour

½ - ¾ cup sugar

1 teaspoon baking powder

¾ teaspoon salt

1 egg

2 tablespoons brown sugar

1 teaspoon cinnamon/sugar

4 cups fresh blueberries

3 cups peeled and sliced tart apples

Splash of lemon juice

⅓ cup melted butter

Preheat oven to 350 degrees.

Sprinkle brown sugar and cinnamon/sugar and lemon juice over apples and berries, and place in buttered 2-quart baking dish.

With a fork, mix sugar, salt, baking powder, unbeaten egg, and flour until roughly blended. Crumble mixture over the fruit in the baking dish, and dribble the melted butter on the top. Bake for 30 minutes or until lightly browned and fruit is bubbling.

BUTTERMILK CAKE WITH MAPLE SEA FOAM ICING

Although this recipe was in my first book, there was a typo in the icing recipe, and I want my readers to have success with their baking.

This was my sister-in-law, Marilyn Stein's signature dessert for every occasion; and even if there wasn't a specific reason to party, this cake appeared and there was an instant celebration!

2 sticks butter

2 cups sugar

2 eggs

2 teaspoons baking soda

1½ cups buttermilk

3 cups cake flour, sifted

1 tablespoon vanilla

MAPLE SEA FOAM ICING:

½ cup water

2 cups brown sugar

4 egg whites

1 tablespoon vanilla

1 tablespoon maple flavoring

Cream butter and sugar until light in color, then add eggs and continue beating until thoroughly mixed.

Dissolve baking soda in buttermilk and add to creamed mixture alternating with the flour. Beat on lowest speed just until flour is mixed through. Blend in vanilla. Bake in 3, greased and floured 9-inch pans. Bake at 350 degrees, 28–33 minutes until toothpick comes out clean.

For maple sea foam icing:

Bring water to a boil. Add sugar and stir until water returns to vigorous boil. In a large mixing bowl beat egg whites until very stiff. Continue beating on high speed and very slowly drizzle boiling sugar mixture down outer edge of bowl. Add vanilla and maples flavorings. Beat until all liquid has been added and stiff peaks form. The addition of the liquid will deflate the egg whites somewhat, however they will come back to peaks with beating. Once cake is iced, it is best served same day.

CAPPUCCINO BROWNIE CAKE

This is one of my all-time favorite brownie recipes. I got it out of Gourmet magazine about 20 years ago, and I've been relying on it ever since. The original recipe calls for an 8-inch square pan, cut into small brownies. However, I prefer to make it as a cake in an 8-inch round spring form pan, and use a fork to eat it; also, this presents a more elegant dessert. It's the combination of chocolate, coffee, and cinnamon that gets to me!

4 ounces bittersweet chocolate, chopped

6 tablespoons unsalted butter

1 tablespoon instant espresso powder, dissolved in

½ tablespoon boiling water

¾ cup sugar

1 teaspoon vanilla

2 large eggs

½ cup flour

¼ teaspoon salt

½ cup walnuts, chopped

CREAM CHEESE FROSTING:

4 ounces cream cheese

3 tablespoons unsalted butter

¾ cup confectioners' sugar, sifted

½ teaspoon vanilla

½ teaspoon cinnamon

GLAZE:

3 ounces bittersweet chocolate

1 tablespoon unsalted butter

¼ cup heavy cream

2¼ teaspoons instant espresso powder, dissolved in

½ tablespoon boiling water

Preheat oven to 350 degrees.

For brownie layer, melt chocolate, butter, and espresso mixture in microwave. Melt for 1 minute, stir, and microwave for 30 seconds.

Cool mixture to lukewarm, and whisk in vanilla, sugar, and eggs, 1 at a time. Stir in flour and salt until just combined, then stir in walnuts.

Spread batter in greased and floured 8-inch spring form pan, and bake for 25 minutes until done. Cool brownie layer completely.

Make frosting in mixer. Beat cream cheese and butter until light and fluffy. Add confectioners' sugar, vanilla, and cinnamon, and beat until well combined. Spread frosting over brownie layer, and chill for 1 hour.

To make the glaze, melt the chocolate and butter with the cream and espresso mixture in the microwave in 30-second increments. Cool glaze, and spread carefully over the chilled brownies. Cover pan, and refrigerate for 3 hours. Remove from pan while still cold before cutting into very thin wedges and plating. Serve cold or at room temperature.

*I freeze each layer before adding the next; then after I put the glaze on, I cool in fridge and then wrap the cake and freeze until ready to use.

"CHEESE DANISH" BUNDT CAKE

Ellen Gersh brought this to a "Break Fast", and it reminded me of a cheese Danish—thus the name!

½ cup butter

1 teaspoon vanilla

2 cups sifted flour

1 teaspoon baking powder

1 teaspoon baking soda

½ pint sour cream

¾ cup sugar

3 eggs

FILLING:

2 (8 ounce) packages cream cheese

¾ cup sugar

1 egg yolk

1 teaspoon vanilla

1 teaspoon lemon juice

Powdered sugar for sifting over cooled cake

Cream butter and sugar together. Add rest of ingredients, and mix well.

Preheat oven to 350 degrees.

Grease bundt pan and put in half the batter.

Beat all filling ingredients together.

Add the entire filling on top of the batter and then cover with the rest of the batter, and bake for 45 minutes.

Cool, then turn out onto a platter. Sift powdered sugar over the top of cake.

CHOCOLATE MOUSSE

Barbara Cohen often makes this mousse for holidays. It's a recipe from her homeland, England. Prepare this the day before planning to serve. It also will freeze well, always a bonus!

Serves 4–6

4 ounces semisweet chocolate

4 large eggs, separated

2 teaspoons instant coffee, dissolved in 3 teaspoons hot water

1½ tablespoons Tia Maria or other coffee or chocolate-flavored liqueur

3 teaspoons sugar

Melt the chocolate in the microwave, 30–60 seconds. When chocolate is melted, immediately drop in the egg yolks and whisk vigorously until mixture begins to thicken. Stir in the coffee and the liqueur. Chill until mixture is quite cool. Beat the egg whites in a mixer until soft peaks form; then add the sugar, and beat until thoroughly mixed. Pour the chocolate into the egg white bowl, and fold through until blended. This can then be put into 8 soufflé dessert dishes or placed in a serving bowl. Leave to chill overnight.

COCONUT CAKE

This delicate white cake is from an old Youngstown Rodef Sholom cookbook. Jeanne Fibus sent it to me, but I also remember Louise Kannensohn's mother, Fran Millstone, making this every year for Louise's New Year's Day birthday. So glad to find this.

¼ pound plus 1 tablespoon butter

1½ cups sugar

2¾ cups cake flour

2¾ teaspoons baking powder

1¼ cups ice water

4 egg whites

1 teaspoon vanilla

COCONUT ICING:

1½ cups sugar

½ cup water, scant

3 egg whites

1 teaspoon vanilla

1 package sweetened coconut flakes to use as needed

Preheat oven to 325 degrees.

Sift flour and baking powder together 3 times and set aside. Cream butter and sugar. Alternately add flour and ice water to butter mixture. Beat egg whites and vanilla until stiff peaks form. Fold the egg whites into the cake batter. Butter 2 round cake pans, and pour batter evenly into each.

Bake at 325 degrees for 10 minutes; then increase heat to 350 degrees for another 15 minutes. Do not over bake! Cool cakes and remove from pans.

For coconut icing: Boil sugar and water together until syrup forms a thread from edge of fork. Beat egg white until stiff, but not too dry. Add 3 tablespoons of the sugar syrup, and mix at high speed. Very gradually, while mixer is running, add balance of syrup and vanilla. Beat until thick and marshmallowy. Frost cake, and sprinkle with coconut.

FRUIT GRATIN

Another super recipe from Sandy Roth.

Serves 6–8

8 cups strawberries

2 cups Greek yogurt

3–4 tablespoons milk or half and half

Pinch of salt

2 teaspoons vanilla

3–4 tablespoons lemon juice

Stevia to taste

Brown sugar

Slice strawberries. Spread out in 9×13 inch oven-proof dish or individual baking dishes.

Whisk together yogurt and milk.

Whisk in juice, vanilla, salt, and Stevia to taste.

Pour yogurt mixture over fruit, and sprinkle with brown sugar.

Broil on rack 1 level down from top for 3 minutes or until sugar melts.

HONEY CAKE

This is Bob Subin's mother's recipe, and he always wants some when I make it.

2¼ cups flour

1 teaspoon baking soda

1 teaspoon baking powder

1 cup dark brown sugar

1 cup honey

½ cup vegetable oil

¼ cup cooled strong coffee

2 eggs

1 teaspoon cinnamon

1 teaspoon ginger

½ teaspoon cloves

½ teaspoon nutmeg

½ teaspoon allspice

Preheat oven to 350 degrees.

Sift flour, baking powder, and baking soda together, and set aside. In a mixing bowl, add all the rest of ingredients, and beat on medium to blend totally. Add sifted ingredients, and mix thoroughly. Pour batter into a greased 5x9 inch loaf pan, and bake for 45 minutes to 1 hour. This batter can also be poured into three 7 ½x3 ¾ inch pans. Check these cakes after ½ hour.

KUMQUATS IN SYRUP

Audrey Miller prepares a beautiful table and always has a deliciously surprising finish to the meal. This time she served these kumquats over ice cream. The good thing is the kumquats will last in the fridge for a few weeks and with some ice cream in the freezer, spontaneous treats are easily offered!

Serves 8 as a sauce over ice cream

1 cup sugar

1 cup water

1½ teaspoons lemon juice

1 pint (2 cups) kumquats

Prepare kumquats:

Thoroughly wash and dry the fruit. Knife an X into the top and bottom, and set aside.

Bring water and sugar to a boil until sugar dissolves, and then reduce heat and simmer, uncovered for 2 minutes. Remove from heat, and add the lemon juice. When the syrup is lukewarm, add the kumquats to the pot and simmer for 10–12 minutes, stirring occasionally until tender. Remove kumquats from the syrup and lightly boil the syrup until it is reduced to almost a thin, gel-like consistency. This may take 10 minutes or so. Cool and put kumquats back into the syrup. Refrigerate until ready to use.

LEMON CAKE

I make this cake in 3 small loaf pans and freeze them, and then I always have a special dessert when I need it. I like it served with some fresh blueberries on the side. Thank you "Barefoot Contessa"! This makes good use of the lemons Louise and Bill Warshauer give me from their bountiful harvest.

½ pound (2 sticks) unsalted butter, at room temperature

2½ cups granulated sugar, divided

4 extra-large eggs, at room temperature

⅓ cup grated lemon zest (6–8 large lemons)

3 cups flour

½ teaspoon baking powder

½ teaspoon baking soda

1 teaspoon kosher salt

¾ cup freshly squeezed lemon juice, divided

¾ cup buttermilk, at room temperature

1 teaspoon pure vanilla extract

FOR THE GLAZE:

2 cups confectioners' sugar, sifted

3½ tablespoons freshly squeezed lemon juice

Preheat the oven to 350 degrees.

Grease and flour two 8×4 inch loaf pans, or use 3 smaller ones (7½×3¾ inch). Line the bottom of the pans with parchment; it makes it so much easier to get the cake out.

Cream the butter and 2 cups granulated sugar in the bowl of an electric mixer fitted with the paddle attachment, until light and fluffy, about 5 minutes. With the mixer on medium speed, add the eggs, 1 at a time, and the lemon zest.

Sift together the flour, baking powder, baking soda, and salt in a bowl. In another bowl, combine ¼ cup lemon juice, the buttermilk, and vanilla. Add the flour and buttermilk mixtures alternately to the batter, beginning and ending with the flour. Divide the batter evenly between the pans, smooth the tops, and bake for 45 minutes to 1 hour, until a cake tester comes out clean.

Combine ½ cup granulated sugar with ½ cup lemon juice in a small saucepan, and cook over low heat until the sugar dissolves. When the cakes are done, allow cooling for 10 minutes. Remove the cakes from the pans and set them on a rack set over a tray or sheet pan; spoon the lemon syrup over them. Allow the cakes to cool completely.

For the glaze, combine the confectioners' sugar and the lemon juice in a bowl, mixing with a wire whisk until smooth. Pour over the tops of the cakes and allow the glaze to drizzle down the sides.

LORNA DOONE SHORTBREAD CAKE WITH HEATH BAR TOPPING

Bobbie Myers took this dessert, a reliable favorite of hers, to Thanksgiving dinner. It's rich, so just a small piece will suffice. This should be prepared early on the day of serving or the day before.

Serves 12

1 package Lorna Doone Shortbread Cookies, finely crushed

1 stick butter, melted

2 small packages vanilla instant pudding

1½ cups milk

1 quart vanilla ice cream, softened

1 (16 ounce) container Cool Whip

2 Heath Bars, crushed, or 1 package Heath Bar Bits

Preheat oven to 350 degrees.

Place cookies in processor, and whir until finely crushed. Combine the crumbs with the melted butter, and press evenly into a 9×13 inch baking dish. Bake for 15 minutes or until lightly browned. Cool completely.

In large mixing bowl, mix both packages of pudding with the milk until thoroughly combined, and then add the ice cream. Pour, and spread evenly over the cooled crust. Spread Cool Whip over pudding mixture and sprinkle with Heath bits. Refrigerate 4 to 24 hours.

PEACH PIE

This is from Nora Ephron's book Heartburn. It's a fun read, and she interspersed her story, basically her split from Carl Bernstein, with recipes. The pie crust alone is worth the recipe! Actually, I tested the recipe and took it over to Anita and Dick Shapiro's, where 5 of us, Kannensohns, too, polished off the entire pie after eating a full meal! But then we all started talking about what our mothers did with the leftover pie crust. Mine always sprinkled cinnamon and sugar over it, and those baked scraps fresh out of the oven were heavenly!

3 peaches, peeled and sliced, or 12 ounces of unsweetened frozen sliced peaches

3 egg yolks

1¼ cups flour, plus 2 tablespoons

1 cup sugar

½ teaspoon salt

¼ cup butter

⅓ cup sour cream, plus 2 tablespoons

Cinnamon and sugar, for sprinkling (optional)

Put the salt, butter, 1¼ cups flour, and 2 tablespoons sour cream in food processor and pulse until ball forms; then pat into buttered pie tin.

Bake at 425 degrees for 10 minutes.

Beat 3 egg yolks slightly and combine with the sugar, 2 remaining tablespoons flour, and ⅓ remaining cup of sour cream.

Pour the egg yolk mixture over 3 peeled and sliced peaches arranged in the crust (When peaches are out of season, I have used 12 ounces of unsweetened frozen sliced peaches. Be sure to thaw and dry them before arranging in crust. However, because it's impossible to get them as dry as fresh peaches, it will take much longer for the filling to set).

Cover with foil. Bake at 350 degrees for 35 minutes. Remove foil. Bake for 10 minutes more until filling is set.

*Sprinkle a bit of cinnamon and sugar over top if you like.

*Reserve egg whites for another use.

PEARS AND STRAWBERRIES IN PORT WINE

Janet and Howard Solot had me to their club for a phenomenal seafood buffet. One of the desserts was an outstanding pear/strawberry compote. This is my version.

4 ripe pears, peeled

2 cups strawberries, hulled

1½ cups port wine

2 packages sugar substitute

Quarter and remove seeds from the pears. Bring the port and Stevia to a boil and poach pears in the liquid. Sugar can be substituted for the Stevia. When the tip of a knife can pierce the pear easily, remove the pears with a slotted spoon to a bowl. Add the strawberries to the liquid, and cook them until they are soft, but still retaining their shape. Remove the strawberries and place in the bowl with the pears. Continue simmering the wine until it is reduced by half. Then pour the liquid over the fruit and bring to room temperature. Serve or store in refrigerator until ready to use.

POACHED PEARS

I get easy, delicious recipes from Barbara Cohen. Her serving style is continental and always distinctive.

Bosc pears — skin on, base sliced flat

1 cup dry red wine — cheap wine will do

⅔ cup sugar

1 teaspoon vanilla

1 cinnamon stick

Slice lemon rind

Preheat oven to 300 degrees.

Place all poaching liquid ingredients in bottom of shallow oven-proof dish, and stir until combined. Place pears, bottoms sliced off so pears will stand upright, in the dish. Bake for 2 hours or until soft but still standing. Baste every so often.

I used Trader Joe's two-buck Chuck Cabernet Sauvignon — it was perfect.

PUMPKIN/CREAM CHEESE LOAF

Janet Solot brought this to a party—it's like pumpkin pie in a cake, with the topping on the inside!

3 loaf pans, sprayed

3 cups sugar

1 can pumpkin (15 ounces)

4 cups flour

1 cup canola oil

1 cup water

4 eggs

4 teaspoons pumpkin pie spice

2 teaspoons baking soda

1½ teaspoons cinnamon

1 teaspoon baking powder

1 teaspoon nutmeg

½ teaspoon ground cloves

1 cup chopped walnuts

1 cup raisins, optional

FILLING:

2 packages cream cheese (8 ounces), softened

1 tablespoon milk

¼ cup sugar

1 egg

For filling, beat cream cheese, ¼ cup sugar, egg, and milk in small bowl.

In large bowl, beat 3 cups sugar, pumpkin, oil, water, and 4 eggs.

Combine dry ingredients. Gradually add to pumpkin mixture. Mix well.

Stir in nuts and raisins (*Janet does one pan without raisins).

Pour ½ batter into 3 pans. Spoon cream cheese over. Cover with remaining batter.

Bake for 1 hour until toothpick comes out clean. Cool 10 minutes. Remove from pan.

Cool completely. Wrap, and refrigerate or freeze.

TOASTED SPICE CAKE

This recipe is from Fanny Spiegle, who was the mother of my sister-in-law, Marilyn's, cousin's husband. Does that show the depth of relationships in Youngstown? Anyway, she was a fabulous baker, and this is definitely a "golden oldie."

1½ cups brown sugar

1 stick butter

3 eggs, 2 separated, 1 whole

1½ cups cake flour

1 teaspoon baking powder

1 teaspoon baking soda

½ teaspoon allspice

½ teaspoon cloves

Pinch salt

1 teaspoon cinnamon

½ cup sour cream

1 teaspoon vanilla

TOPPING:

2 egg whites

1 cup light brown sugar

½ cup walnuts, chopped

Preheat oven to 325 degrees.

Sift together flour, baking soda, baking powder, allspice, cloves, salt, and cinnamon. Set aside.

Beat together brown sugar and butter. Add 2 egg yolks and 1 whole egg. Mix well. Add vanilla to sour cream, and add this to egg mixture alternately with sifted ingredients. Mix after each addition. Pour into greased 9-inch square pan.

Beat 2 egg whites until stiff, and gradually add brown sugar. Spread over batter; sprinkle with the nuts, and bake for 35 minutes.

CANDY AND NUTS

BUCKEYES

Kathy made these for Alex's college graduation party, and all the Ohioans became nostalgic and made them "all gone"!

1 pound butter

2 cups peanut butter

2½ pounds confectioners' sugar

3 teaspoons vanilla

12 ounces chocolate chips

⅛ pound paraffin wax

Cream butter and peanut butter; mix to smooth consistency. Add vanilla and sugar. Form into buckeye-sized balls.

Melt chocolate chips and paraffin in double boiler. Once well heated and thickened, dip balls into chocolate with toothpick, leaving some peanut butter showing to imitate a buckeye. Place on wax paper until chocolate hardens. Layer on wax paper to store. May freeze.

BARBARA HEIMANN

CHOCOLATE-MIXED NUT BARK WITH SEA SALT

This past summer I went into a popular candy store in Sharon, Pennsylvania, and bought some of their chocolate bark to take to a friend's home as a hostess gift. The store charged $18.95 a pound for this. Well, to me, Trader Joe's Belgian chocolate bars are as good as it gets, and each bar is only $4.99! So, I came up with this recipe.

1 (17.6 ounce bar) Trader Joe's milk chocolate

1 (17.6 ounce bar) Trader Joe's 72% dark chocolate

1¼ cups unsalted mixed nuts—cashews, pistachios, and pecans

Coarse sea salt (for sprinkling) no more than a scant teaspoon

Line a 12×15 inch baking sheet with parchment paper.

Coarsely chop nuts.

Break chocolate into squares and place in glass bowl.

Microwave chocolate on high for 2 minutes. Stir and microwave for 1½ minutes more. Stir again so chocolates are thoroughly combined; then pour chocolate into prepared baking sheet—make sure chocolate evenly covers entire pan. Sprinkle nuts over chocolate, and refrigerate for 7 minutes. Just as chocolate is beginning to set, lightly sprinkle sea salt over entire confection. Continue chilling for about 3 hours. Break or cut bark into pieces, and store between layers of parchment or waxed paper.

Do Ahead: Can be made 1 week ahead. Keep chilled.

SUGARED PECANS

These are very easy to make; just be sure to bake them until they are dry. I first had these in 1994 when we had moved to Naples and were invited to Dolly and Bill Turner's condo for dinner. They were new neighbors in St. Kitts, and although I have a hazy memory of the dinner, my best takeaway was this nut recipe, which is so satisfyingly sweet and salty.

1 egg white

1 teaspoon water

3 cups pecan halves

1 teaspoon cinnamon

½ teaspoon salt

¾ cup sugar

Preheat oven to 250 degrees.

Whisk the egg whites and water together until they become a little firm and frothy. And then add the pecans, and stir through the egg white mixture.

Thoroughly combine the cinnamon, salt and sugar.

Mix the spices into the nut mixture, and place on a cookie sheet. Bake at 250 degrees for 45 minutes to 1 hour, until the nuts are dry. Stir the nuts at least once during the baking process. Break apart when nuts are cool, and store in airtight container.

COOKIES

CHOCOLATE CHUNK COOKIES

I got this recipe from The Ritz many years ago when I also got their chocolate chip cookie recipe, which has been made too many times to count.

4 eggs

1½ cups sugar

1 teaspoon vanilla

1 teaspoon instant coffee

12 ounces dark chocolate

4 ounces milk chocolate

¾ cup butter

⅔ cup flour

½ teaspoon baking powder

1 cup walnuts, chopped

1 cup pecans, chopped

Preheat oven to 350 degrees.

Whip together eggs, sugar, vanilla, and coffee until light and fluffy.

Melt the chocolates and butter and combine. Mix into the egg mixture.

Add flour and baking powder; mix well, and add nuts. Chill for 30 minutes.

Scoop onto parchment-lined cookie sheet, and bake in convection oven at 350 degrees for 22 minutes using a ¼ cup scoop. Also, scoops can be frozen before baking, and then you can take out as many cookies as needed. Bake while serving dinner, and serve them warm for dessert! This makes 20 large cookies.

CRANBERRY COOKIES

This recipe comes from Sandy Roth via a column she used to write for the Youngstown Jewish Journal—her nom de plume was Saucy Sandy.

2 cups flour

¼ teaspoon salt

2 tablespoons orange juice

½ teaspoon baking soda

1 teaspoon cinnamon

1 stick butter

1 cup white sugar

¾ cup brown sugar

1 egg

¼ cup milk

1 cup regular oatmeal

12 ounces fresh cranberries

1 cup toasted walnuts

Preheat oven to 350 degrees.

Lightly grease two cookie sheets or line with parchment.

Mix flour, salt, baking soda, and cinnamon into a bowl and set aside. Cream butter and sugars until light and fluffy, and then beat in egg and milk.

Stir flour mixture with orange juice just to combine, and add to butter mixture. Beat thoroughly. Fold in oatmeal, cranberries, and nuts. Drop onto cookie sheets, using soup spoon, 2 inches apart. Bake for 20–25 minutes until edges are golden and cranberries have burst.

Batter can be frozen, and then baked.

CRANBERRY NUT BISCOTTI

This recipe is from JoAnn Roth, who got it from Marisa D'Alesandro. It's an old recipe that's been handed down in Marisa's family and one that hits somewhat healthy notes, as there's no oil and plenty of nuts and cranberries, which are good for you. I'm not a fan of almond flavoring, so I substituted vanilla. The original recipe called for 2 tablespoons almond flavoring; again, I reduced that to 1 tablespoon. Taste the mixture in case you want to add more flavoring. Apparently, the original Italian recipe called for 3 cups of whole almonds. Give that a try!

6 large eggs

2 cups sugar

Pinch salt

1 tablespoon almond flavoring or vanilla

(If using vanilla, add grated rind of ½ lemon)

4 cups flour—can use 1 cup whole wheat and 3 cups white

2 cups cranberries

2 cups walnuts, 1½ cups chopped and ½ cup ground

(Or can use almonds or pistachios)

Preheat oven to 350 degrees.

In mixer beat eggs; then add sugar, salt, and almond flavoring. Beat on medium for 2 minutes. Then add flour, and mix until well combined. Stir in cranberries and then nuts. Refrigerate for ½ hour.

Divide dough into thirds and form each third into a long log. Bake for ½ hour, turning front to back halfway through. Remove from oven and cool for 5 minutes; then slice into ½ -inch slices on an angle. Return to oven for 6 minutes to dry out a bit.

CREAMY RASPBERRY BARS

CRUST:

1¼ cups flour

1 cup oatmeal, any kind

⅔ cup sugar

1 teaspoon baking powder

¼ cup walnuts, finely chopped (optional)

½ cup butter, melted

TOPPING:

1 package cream cheese (8 ounces)

¼ cup plus 1 tablespoon sugar

2 eggs

1 tablespoon lemon juice plus a bit of rind

1 teaspoon vanilla

⅔ cup raspberry preserves

Preheat oven to 375 degrees.

Combine crust ingredients, and press firmly into ungreased 9×13 inch pan. Bake for 15 minutes. Beat cream cheese ingredients together until creamy. Gently spread raspberry preserves over hot crust. Then pour cream cheese mixture over preserves.

Bake 18–20 minutes until cream cheese is set and edges are golden. Cool completely. Cut into bars.

JESSICA'S COOKIE CRACK

When I was in Sharon, for my brother Leon and Shirley Stein's 60th anniversary weekend, we often were sitting around their dining table, looking through the bay window at the gorgeous fall foliage. Of course, there was constant talking and nibbling. Their granddaughter, Jessica Stein, brought these cookies, which slowly and surely got eaten up over the weekend. In fact, when I made them upon my return to Naples, Kay Tamarkin, who has an insatiable sweet tooth, loved them so much she sent me 4 packages of the toffee bits covered in chocolate from Boca, as I couldn't find them in Naples at that time.

1 cup unsalted butter, at room temperature

¾ cup sugar

1½ teaspoons pure vanilla extract

1 teaspoon salt

2 cups all-purpose flour

Sprinkle of cinnamon (optional)

1 cup mini semisweet chocolate chips

8–10 ounces of Heath Milk Chocolate English Toffee Bits

Preheat the oven to 350 degrees.

Cut two sheets of parchment paper the size of each baking sheet and set on counter.

In a large bowl, cream together the butter and sugar until smooth. Add the vanilla and salt. Slowly add the flour, and mix until combined. Stir in the chocolate chips and heath pieces.

Divide the dough in half and place one piece of dough on each sheet of parchment. Using your fingers begin to press the dough flat; then place a sheet of plastic wrap over the dough, and using a rolling pin over the plastic wrap, spread the dough into one evenly thin (¼–⅛ inch) layer. Remove top piece of wrap; then simply place sheet of parchment with dough back into the pan.

Bake 20–25 minutes or until golden brown (in convection oven at 325 degrees on two racks–25 minutes).

Immediately after removing from oven, slice into small squares using a pizza cutter or sharp knife. Cool completely, and then break into the squares.

These freeze well.

KOOKIE BRITTLE

Michelle Kaplan makes her "crack" this quick and simple way! The recipe makes about 1¾ pounds. Kids love it, as do the bridge ladies!

1 cup butter, unsalted

1½ teaspoons vanilla

1 teaspoon salt

1 cup sugar

2 cups flour, sifted

6 ounces mini semisweet chocolate chips

¾ cup finely chopped pecans (optional)

Preheat oven to 375 degrees.

Blend butter, vanilla, and salt. Gradually beat in the sugar. Add 2 cups flour and the chocolate chips. Mix thoroughly.

Press the batter evenly into an ungreased 10×15 inch cookie sheet. Bake at 375 degrees for 20 minutes or until golden brown. I use a pizza cutter to slice through the warm kookie out of the oven. I can easily get small squares. Before separating kookies into pieces, cool completely.

MARSHMALLOW BROWNIES

Myrna Levin and I were at a party talking about my cookbook. I told her I was planning another and asked her for a recipe. This is it, and to paraphrase her words—by adding the mini marshmallows, "magic occurs". Abracadabra!

Makes one 8×8 inch pan

Double recipe for 9×13 inch pan

2 ounces unsweetened chocolate

1 stick of butter

2 eggs

Pinch salt

1 scant cup sugar

½ cup flour

1 teaspoon vanilla

1 cup miniature marshmallows

½ cup semisweet chocolate chips

½ cup pecans

Preheat oven to 350 degrees.

Place butter and chocolate in bowl, and microwave for 1 minute. Stir, and microwave another 30 seconds. If the chocolate is not thoroughly melted, it should melt in the warm butter. Add the next five ingredients; stir until blended; and then add the chips, marshmallows, and nuts.

Place in greased pan, and bake in a 350-degree oven for 25–28 minutes. Cool and enjoy, or freeze for later use.

ORANGE COOKIES

My mother used to make this cake-like cookie, which, when baking, made the house smell like spring was in the air!

Makes 3 dozen cookies

½ cup butter

¾ cup sugar

½ cup sour cream

1 egg

⅓ cup orange juice

2 cups flour

½ teaspoon baking powder

½ teaspoon baking soda

2 tablespoons grated orange peel

FROSTING:

2½ tablespoons butter

1½ tablespoons orange juice

2 tablespoons grated orange rind

1½ cups confectioners' sugar

Preheat oven to 375 degrees.

Combine sugar and butter, and cream. Add sour cream and egg, and blend well.

Add rest of ingredients, and mix thoroughly. Drop by teaspoonful onto parchment-lined cookie sheet. Bake 10–12 minutes.

ORANGE-RICOTTA COOKIES

I was at Saquella one day and I just had to finish off my lunch with some-thing sweet. I love orange cookies, healthy – yes? Well, my waitress was telling me about the ricotta cookies that she loved and how her Italian grandmother always baked with ricotta cheese, and she recommended these cookies. Plan on using 3 oranges!

Makes 3 dozen cookies

2½ cups flour

1 teaspoons baking powder

½ teaspoon salt

½ teaspoon cinnamon

2 tablespoons poppy seeds

1½ cups sugar

2 oranges, zested

2 eggs

½ cup unsalted butter

1 teaspoon vanilla

2 tablespoons orange juice

1 (15 ounce) container ricotta cheese

GLAZE:

1½ cups powdered sugar

3 tablespoons orange juice

1 orange, zested

Preheat oven to 350 degrees.

Combine flour, baking powder, salt, cinnamon and poppy seeds in a bowl and set aside.

In a mixing bowl, combine the sugar with the orange zest and mix well. Add the butter and mix well, and then add the eggs, and mix until well incorporated. Add the vanilla, orange juice and ricotta and mix well. Add the dry ingredients and combine well with the ingredients in the mixer.

Using parchment-lined cookie sheets, scoop 2 tablespoons dough onto baking sheet. You should get about 3 dozen cookies. Bake at 350 degrees for 18–22 minutes until edges are slightly golden. Let cool completely.

Make glaze and spread about 1 teaspoon over each cookie.

BARBARA HEIMANN

PASSOVER COOKIES

My sister-in-law, Brenda Blatt actually makes these year-round and keeps them in her freezer. This is a fabulous flourless cookie and so easy to make.

2 egg whites

1 tablespoon vanilla

⅓ cup sugar (or 3 packages sugar alternative—Truvia, or Splenda)

3 cups chopped slivered almonds, pine nuts, dried cranberries, chocolate chips, butterscotch bits, etc.

Preheat oven to 350 degrees.

Line cookie sheet with parchment paper.

Whisk egg whites and vanilla just until frothy. Add the assortment of nuts, berries, and chips, and mix through. Finally stir in sugar or sweetener. Drop by tablespoons onto cookie sheet. Bake for 13 minutes.

PASSOVER COOKIES (MY VERSION)

I made these last night with odds and ends of packages I had in my pantry, and this is my version. There were only a few cookies left, which I sent home with a guest.

2 egg whites

1 teaspoon vanilla

Slivered almonds, coconut, chocolate chips, pine nuts, pecans, and cranberries (all chopped): enough to total 3 cups, individual amounts as desired.

½ cup sugar

1 teaspoon cinnamon

¼ teaspoon salt

Preheat convection oven to 325 degrees.

Whisk egg whites and vanilla. Stir in nut mixture. Sift sugar, cinnamon, and salt into mixture. Use a 1-tablespoon measure to form 30 cookies. Bake at 325 degrees convection for 12–13 minutes.

PEANUT BUTTER CHOCOLATE CHUNK BARS

Very easy—very good!

1½ cups flour

½ teaspoon baking soda

¾ cup brown sugar

¾ cup creamy peanut butter

1 stick butter, room temperature

½ cup granulated sugar

1 egg

1 teaspoon vanilla

1 package (11½ ounces) semisweet chocolate chunks

Preheat oven to 350 degrees.

Beat sugars, butter, and peanut butter until creamy. Add egg and vanilla. Gradually add flour/soda mixture until all is combined. Stir in chunks. Press into ungreased 9×13 inch pan. Bake for 20–25 minutes until lightly browned. Cool completely, and cut into bars.

PECAN PUFFS

Marlene Epstein graciously brings these scrumptious cookies when visiting a house of gladness or sadness—celebratory or comforting. Be prepared to eat more than one!

Makes 20 cookies

½ cup butter (Marlene uses salted butter)

¼ cup sugar

1 teaspoon vanilla

1 cup flour

1 cup pecans halves, broken into pieces*

½ cup confectioners' sugar, sifted

Preheat oven to 300 degrees.

Cream butter and sugar, and add vanilla. (The creaming process can be done using a hand mixer or a food processor.) Mix until light and creamy. Stir in flour and then pecans, and blend thoroughly. Roll into 20 walnut size balls.

Place on greased baking sheets, or parchment paper, and bake for 30 minutes. Check after 25 minutes. Remove from oven and roll in powdered sugar while still warm. These freeze well. After freezing, however, dust the cookies once more with powdered sugar.

*Pecans can be toasted beforehand if you prefer.

RASPBERRY CHEESECAKE BROWNIES

This is a recipe from Chef George Duran that I saw in a magazine. These freeze well.

2 cups frozen raspberries, thawed

1 (8 ounce) package cream cheese, room temperature

½ cup sugar

1 egg

2 tablespoons flour

1 (18–20 ounce) package brownie mix

Preheat oven to 350 degrees.

Puree raspberries in blender, and then strain over a bowl. Press the raspberries through the strainer, leaving the seeds behind.

Then combine ⅓ cup raspberry sauce with the cream cheese, sugar, egg, and flour in mixer, and mix until completely smooth.

In a separate bowl, make brownie mix according to package directions.

Grease a 9×13 inch pan, and pour ⅔ of brownie mixture into pan. Top with raspberry mixture, and spread gently. Add the remaining brownie mix in dollops. Use a knife through batter to make swirls so the batter looks marbleized.

Bake for 30–35 minutes. Cool, and cut into squares.

RASPBERRY PILLOWS

JoAnn Roth makes these and calls them "cookies from hell" as they're absolutely sinfully delicious. I do believe "gluttony" falls into the sinful category—one will just not do!

DOUGH:

2 sticks butter

8 ounces cream cheese

½ teaspoon vanilla

2¼ cups flour

Powdered sugar

FILLING:

1 can Solo raspberry filling

½ cup walnuts, chopped

Pulse butter and cream cheese with the flour in the food processor. When the dough comes together, process some more until it forms a tight ball. Refrigerate the dough until cold before proceeding with the recipe or freeze at this point. Place some powdered sugar on surface; then roll out dough on the powdered sugar into a rectangle ¼ inch thick. Cut dough into 3-inch squares, and place some of the filling on top, leaving a small border. Fold, envelope style—sides in, and then roll up.

Bake at 375 degrees for 14 minutes. When cool, roll in powdered sugar. These can be frozen, but after defrosting, dust with a bit more powdered sugar.

RUGELACH

Pat Cohen makes these so beautifully that when mine don't turn out as perfectly I wonder what I'm doing wrong. Nevertheless, they are a delicious mouthful in any case! This recipe doubles easily and freezes very well, so just make a double batch and be done with it! Pull them out of the freezer as needed!

DOUGH:

½ pound cream cheese, room temperature

2 sticks unsalted butter, room temperature

2 cups flour

2 tablespoons sugar

FILLING:

12 ounces apricot jam, not preserves, or can use raspberry jam

½ cup sugar mixed with 1 tablespoon cinnamon

½ cup ground pecans

½ cup dried currants, optional

The dough can be mixed by hand, in a Cuisinart, or a mixer. However, don't overwork the dough! Divide the dough into 6 balls. Roll each ball into an 8-inch circle on a piece of waxed paper. Stack each paper with dough, one on top of the other. Cover, and refrigerate overnight or until dough is cold.

Preheat oven to 375 degrees.

Take out one sheet of the dough, and transfer to a floured cutting board.

Cut dough in half and then into quarters (you will have 8 sections of dough). Cut each quarter into four. Spread lightly with jam. Sprinkle 1½ tablespoons cinnamon/sugar mixture over. Sprinkle pecans and/or currants. Quickly roll each 4th from the outside toward the center. Place on a parchment-lined cookie sheet. Continue until all dough is used.

STRUDEL BITES

3 dozen

2 cups flour

8 ounces cream cheese, cut into 8 pieces, room temperature

8 ounces butter, cut into 8 pieces, room temperature

6 tablespoons apricot preserves, divided

6 tablespoons seedless raspberry preserves, divided

Cinnamon/sugar mixture

6 tablespoons chopped walnuts, divided

6 tablespoons raisins, divided

6 tablespoons sweetened coconut, divided

6 teaspoons sour cream, divided

In food processor, place flour, cream cheese, and butter. Pulse until all is incorporated; then run until ingredients form into a ball. Remove dough; mix through by hand to make sure there are no lumps of butter or cream cheese. Then form into a flat round, and wrap in plastic wrap. Refrigerate until thoroughly cold or overnight.

When ready to prepare, preheat oven to 375 degrees.

Remove dough from fridge and allow warming up a bit for 10 minutes. Divide dough into 6 equal parts. On a piece of parchment paper, roll out one part into a rectangle, as thinly as possible. With such rich dough, I like to place a piece of waxed paper over the dough and then use rolling pin over the paper. The dough should roll out to about 5×9 inches. Spread 2 tablespoons preserves over dough.

Half the strudels will be apricot; half will be raspberry. Sprinkle each with cinnamon and sugar. Then sprinkle on 1 tablespoon each of walnuts, raisins, and coconut.

Roll the dough up lengthwise, using the parchment paper as help. Repeat this process with the other 5 pieces of dough.

Transfer rolls, seam side down on parchment-lined baking sheet. Brush top of each roll with 1 teaspoon sour cream.

Bake for 30–35 minutes until golden. It takes the full 35 minutes in my oven. Cool, and then slice into 1-inch bite-size strudels. I use a serrated knife to make the initial cut, and then use a sharp chef's knife to finish.

MEAT

STUFFED PEPPERS

BAKED BEANS WITH SALAMI

This is such an easy side dish for a barbecue. Because it has salami in it, it's a good combo with some grilled chicken; a salad, cookies, and you have a party!

1 can lima beans, drained and rinsed

1 can butter beans, drained and rinsed

1 can kidney beans, drained and rinsed

1 can vegetarian baked beans

¾ cup brown sugar

¼ cup cider vinegar

1 clove garlic, minced

4 large onions, chopped

1 teaspoon dry mustard

2 tablespoons molasses

½ cup catsup

½ teaspoon salt

½ pound salami, cubed, or

½ pound kosher hot dogs

Combine brown sugar, vinegar, garlic, onions, mustard, molasses, and catsup, and simmer 15 minutes. Add beans and salami, and mix well. Pour into 3-quart casserole, and bake at 350 degrees for 1 hour.

BEEF SANDWICHES WITH BLUE CHEESE DRESSING

This is a tasty way to serve thin slices of grilled steak or fillet of beef. With good crusty bread, the beef and dressing will make a great sandwich. Alternatively, I like to serve room temperature grilled steak alongside a gorgeous fresh salad with the dressing on the side.

DRESSING:

¼ pound creamy blue cheese

⅔ cup sour cream

⅓ cup mayonnaise

1½ teaspoons Worcestershire sauce

1 teaspoon kosher salt

1 teaspoon freshly ground black pepper

Mash the blue cheese, and blend in all the other ingredients.

BRISKET

This brisket has a tangy, sweet and sour flavor. I like to make my brisket a day ahead of serving. After it is cooked and cooled, I drain off the sauce into a jar; then slice the brisket, and refrigerate until ready to use. Before reheating, remove the fat that has congealed off the top of the sauce, and pour the fat-free sauce over the sliced brisket.

3½ pounds brisket, first cut

1½ teaspoons salt

Pepper, freshly ground

½ teaspoon garlic powder

Paprika

1 (12 ounce) bottle chili sauce

¼ cup water

¼ cup cider vinegar

½ cup plus 1 tablespoons dark brown sugar, separated

1 teaspoon Worcestershire sauce

2 Vidalia onions, thinly sliced

Rub brisket on both sides with salt, pepper, garlic powder, paprika, and 1 tablespoon brown sugar.

Simmer chili sauce, water, vinegar, sugar, and Worcestershire on stove just long enough to melt the sugar and blend the flavors. Taste, and add more sugar or Worcestershire if you like.

Place half the sliced onions in the bottom of a roasting pan. Top the onions with the seasoned brisket. Place remaining onions on top of brisket, and pour the sauce over all.

Bake covered at 400 degrees for 30 minutes, and then reduce heat to 350 degrees until done, about 2½ hours more.

*If making a whole brisket, use three onions. Do not double the vinegar in the sauce. If doubling, only add 2 more tablespoons of vinegar. The amount of sauce for a single recipe probably will do for a whole brisket; just slice the extra onion.

BRISKET IN CHIPOTLE-MAPLE BARBEQUE SAUCE

I had my Youngstown group over. They were invited to come hungry and thirsty. To me, that indicated a hearty main course. I found this recipe in a book that I like very much—Sarah Foster's "Fresh Every Day." I served this brisket with slider buns, caramelized onions, a big tossed salad, braised cabbage, and a vinaigrette potato salad. The Chipotle Barbeque Sauce is such a favorite of mine that I make it to keep in the fridge and use over chicken or ribs.

1 (4 pounds) beef brisket

2 tablespoons rub (recipe follows)

½ cup light brown sugar

¼ cup Worcestershire sauce

2 tablespoons balsamic vinegar

1 cup barbecue sauce (recipe follows) or can use favorite bought sauce

1 cup beer

RUB:

2 tablespoons paprika

1 tablespoon black pepper

1 tablespoon kosher salt

1 tablespoon garlic powder

1 tablespoon chili powder

1 tablespoon brown sugar

¼ teaspoon cayenne pepper

121

CHIPOTLE-MAPLE BARBECUE SAUCE:

1 (28 ounce) can crushed tomatoes

½ cup maple syrup

½ cup light brown sugar

1–2 chipotle peppers in adobe sauce, diced

¾ cup white vinegar

¼ cup Worcestershire sauce

½ cup apple juice

Juice of 2 lemons

4 cloves garlic, minced

2 tablespoons dry mustard

2 teaspoons sea salt

2 teaspoons black pepper

For the rub: Combine all. This will keep for a few months in fridge.

Use the rub to massage into the room temperature brisket. Stir next three ingredients together, and pour over the brisket, making sure brisket is covered on all sides. Cover, and marinate overnight.

Next day, fire up the outdoor grill. Remove meat from marinade and sear on the grill 4–6 minutes a side until outside is slightly charred. This can be refrigerated at this point until ready to bake the brisket.

Preheat oven to 350 degrees. Place charred brisket in pan, and pour reserved marinade over it. Then stir the barbecue sauce and beer together, and pour that all over the brisket. Cover, and bake for approximately 3½ hours or 4 hours for 8-pound brisket.

Slice, and pour juices over. Serve with additional warm barbecue sauce.

*Chipotle-maple barbecue sauce: For the peppers, just start with one. You can always add more to taste. Combine all ingredients in saucepan, bring to a boil, and then reduce heat and simmer for ½ hour. Sauce will keep in fridge for a few weeks.

CHILI-RUBBED RIBS WITH ESPRESSO BARBEQUE SAUCE

I like the fact that the preparation and cooking can be done even a day ahead; then all that needs to be done is throw them on the grill before serving to get a nice char and smoky flavor.

Serves 4

4 pounds ribs, baby backs, or cross-cut beef short rib flanken—your choice

1 (12 ounce) bottle dark beer

RUB:

2 tablespoons hot Mexican-style chili powder or regular chili powder with a dash of cayenne

1 tablespoon paprika

1 tablespoon ground cumin

1½ teaspoons salt

¾ teaspoon black pepper

ESPRESSO BARBEQUE SAUCE:

1 (18 ounce) bottle BBQ sauce—"Bone Suckin" thicker style works well

½ cup water

2 tablespoons golden brown sugar

1 tablespoon instant espresso

Preheat oven to 400 degrees.

Mix all rub ingredients together. Place ribs in a large roasting pan, and rub the spice mixture all over the ribs. If serving more than four, figure 1-pound rib per person, and adjust other ingredients accordingly. Simmer the beer until reduced to one cup; careful this doesn't boil over! Then pour beer around ribs in the roaster. Cover the pan tightly with foil, and bake for 1½ hours at 400 degrees. Remove ribs from roaster, and cool. Discard liquid. This can be done a day before serving. The sauce can be done ahead of time also.

Bring to room temperature before grilling. And then brush some of the sauce on the ribs and grill to get a nice outdoorsy flavor on them and to give them a good char. Gently heat the sauce, and serve as an accompaniment to the ribs.

EMPANADAS

I met Leonor Macchi at a brunch, and we got to talking about what food she would be preparing for Xmas. She is Argentinian and was definitely going to make these empanadas for her family.

Makes 30

3 packages Goya frozen empanada disks, defrosted

1 pound chopped sirloin

1 bag frozen chopped onions

1 large potato, cooked, and cut into small pieces

3 hard-boiled eggs, chopped

2 carrots, cooked and chopped

Condiments to taste: paprika, salt, white pepper, black pepper, and cumin

You can also add raisins and or chopped olives and a few splashes of olive oil.

Preheat oven to 400 degrees.

Sauté onions in olive oil until lightly browned. Add beef, and cook for about 15 minutes, stirring occasionally. Remove from heat. Add condiments, and cool.

Add remaining ingredients: potato, carrots, and eggs.

Place a tablespoon of mix in center of disk, wet edges with water, and fold together so it looks like a half moon. Press edge of semicircle with a fork to seal well.

Place empanadas on parchment-lined cookie sheets, and bake until golden brown.

EYE OF ROUND ROAST WITH COFFEE RUB

This recipe caught my eye—excuse the pun—because of the unusual rub. This is an inexpensive way to have roast beef on hand for delicious open-face baguette sandwiches or sliced in strips over a salad. Prepare one day ahead; then chill overnight. The cooking time is perfect!

Serves 8–10

Eye of round roast (3 pounds) or bottom round

HERE'S THE RUB!

¼ cup grated onion

2 tablespoons instant coffee

2 teaspoons grated orange rind

2 tablespoons orange juice

1½ tablespoons chili powder

1½ teaspoons kosher salt

3 cloves garlic, minced

1 teaspoon vegetable oil

Preheat oven to 475 degrees.

Combine all the rub ingredients and slather over roast. Place roast in pan just large enough to fit. Place in hot oven for 20 minutes; then turn oven down to 300 degrees, and continue roasting for another 30 minutes. Remove from oven and cool, and then refrigerate overnight. The next day, slice as thinly as possible. Serve on favorite bread, with some horseradish sauce or savory mustard.

*I tested in a convection oven, thus preheated to 450 degrees, and then turned down to 275 degrees.

MEATBALLS FOR CURRY SAUCE

This recipe comes from Jenelle Buza, a Ritz Carleton chef in Naples. She's a great teacher and works very hard on her recipes. The meatball recipe for the curry is hers with a slight variation from me. Her curry sauce is also wonderful over boneless chicken breasts.

1 pound ground beef, 85% lean

1 jalapeño, seeded and minced

1 tablespoon ground ginger

1 large clove garlic, minced

½ cup cooked rice

1 egg

1 tablespoon cilantro, chopped

1 teaspoon Garam Masala

Salt and pepper

Combine all ingredients. Form into meatballs and either brown on stovetop or roast in 400-degree oven for 10–12 minutes. Then prepare as in directions for curry sauce.

CURRY SAUCE

5 Roma tomatoes, chopped

¼ teaspoon sugar

½ large onion, diced

1 large clove garlic, minced

1 teaspoon ground ginger

1 teaspoon ground cumin

1 tablespoon Garam Masala

1½ teaspoons ground Turmeric

1 teaspoon paprika

½ teaspoon chili powder

1 (14 ounce) can coconut milk

Dash cayenne

Salt and pepper

Sauté onions until translucent; add garlic, and stir through onion. Add chopped tomatoes and sugar. Cook for 5 minutes or until tomatoes release their juices. Add rest of the spices, and cook for 3 minutes more. Pour in the coconut milk, and simmer for 25 minutes. Add salt and pepper to taste. Serve over meatballs. Can be done ahead. Pour some of the sauce over cooked meatballs so they get the full flavor of the sauce. Serve remaining sauce on the side.

PRIME RIB

I'm always looking for new methods to make an old stand-by. I came across this recipe from The Spruce, which is a bit different from the closed-oven methods I've seen before. I tested this using a rib eye roast, although I would have preferred using the prime rib on the bone as the bones add so much flavor. I figured out the timing, and the roast came out very well browned, but just a bit more done than I would like. I'm a very "rare" woman! That being said, I tried this again as perhaps my oven wasn't exactly calibrated. So then, I got a standing rib roast, and I re-calibrated the oven. The result was just as I had hoped—perfect!

1 boneless or bone-in rib roast

Salt and pepper to taste

Refrigerate roast 1 day ahead

The night before planning to serve roast, place it uncovered in the fridge. This will dry it out and result in a nice brown crust.

Three hours before cooking remove from fridge and bring to room temperature.

Preheat oven to 500 degrees for 30 minutes before starting the roasting.

Place roast on a rack in a shallow pan, and season generously with salt and pepper.

Multiply the weight of the roast by 5. Thus a 4-pound roast = 20 minutes.

When ready to cook, place roast in hot oven, and roast for amount of time you calculated. When the time is up, turn the oven off and roast for another 2 hours. Do not open oven door!

When time is up, remove from oven; carve, and serve. No need to rest the meat.

RACK OF LAMB

Bruce was in Naples for a few days, and he always likes to spend time with his, and my, friends, Lynni and Peter Mendelson. When Bruce was making plans with them, I suggested that they just come here for dinner as I had two racks of lamb in the freezer, which I wanted to use. As it turned out, this is probably the easiest dinner to prepare with results that are impressive and consistently good! One rack serves 2 people. To serve more, just double or triple the recipe. You can use dried herbs for this.

1 (1½–2 pound) rack of lamb, Frenched

MARINADE:

1 tablespoon Dijon mustard

1–2 cloves garlic, minced

2 teaspoons thyme

1 tablespoon rosemary, crushed

1 teaspoon Worcestershire

2 tablespoons olive oil

Preheat oven to 450 degrees.

Trim excess fat from lamb rack if needed.

Make a paste of all the marinade ingredients. Rub the paste all over both sides and ends of lamb. Cover, and refrigerate overnight. Bring to room temperature before roasting.

Place rack of lamb, rack side down in low-sided roasting pan. Place in upper third of oven. Roast for 25 minutes. Remove from oven, tent with foil, and let rest for 10–15 minutes. Cut into perfectly medium-rare chops, and serve.

REUBEN SANDWICH

Donna and Marc Stein's sons, David and Michael, give this recipe an A+.
Donna can't make enough of them!

Serves 6

1 package crescent rolls

½ pound corned beef, chopped

1 cup sauerkraut, squeezed dry

½ pound Swiss cheese, shredded

¼ cup Thousand Island dressing

2 tablespoons Dijon mustard

1 egg white

1 teaspoon caraway seeds

Preheat oven to 350 degrees.

Mix corned beef with sauerkraut and Swiss cheese, and then combine the beef mixture with the combined dressing/mustard mixture.

Lay out the crescent rolls into a rectangle. Place Reuben mixture down the middle of the rectangle. Cut dough at either side into angled strips. Place strips, alternating in a braided fashion. Brush top of sandwich with egg white and sprinkle caraway seeds over it. Bake at 350 degrees for 20–25 minutes.

STUFFED PEPPERS ITALIAN STYLE

This recipe comes from the Youngstown Angels and Friends cookbook, and it is a favorite from Rich Alberini's eponymous restaurant in the area. JoAnn Roth has made some revisions to the original recipe. This dish is a favorite of hers as part of a menu for a buffet dinner. She also prepares ahead by stuffing the peppers; then freezing them. When wanting to serve them, she simply places the frozen peppers on a baking pan, brushes them with some oil, and proceeds to bake them according to the recipe.

3 cups bread crumbs from a stale loaf

1 pound Italian sausage, can use chicken variety

½ cup Parmesan, grated

1 egg, beaten

¼ cup Italian parsley, chopped

¼ cup olive oil

6 cloves garlic, smashed

16–20 cubanelle peppers

Cut the tops off the peppers; discard the stems, membranes, and seeds.

Trim crust from bread, and cube the bread. Then place in food processor and pulse until fine breadcrumb stage. Set aside.

Filling: Sauté the garlic in the olive oil. Cool and then remove the garlic. Brown the sausage in the garlic oil, mashing it to make it fine.

Combine the breadcrumbs, Parmesan, sausage, and parsley. If needed, add a bit more olive oil until this mixture is moist. Add egg to this mixture. Stuff the peppers and place them in a casserole dish. Drizzle a small amount of oil over the peppers. Cover with foil, and bake at 350 degrees for 45 minutes to 1 hour. Remove foil last 15 minutes of cooking.

*I was testing this recipe and couldn't find cubanelle peppers, so this is what I came up with. I had three friends over to eat the results, and all deemed the recipe a "keeper."

4 red bell peppers cut in half through stem, seeds and membrane removed

1 pound chicken sausage (⅔ mild sausage, ⅓ hot sausage)

1½ cups breadcrumbs (⅔ challah, ⅓ ciabatta)

½ cup Parmesan, grated

1 egg, beaten

¼ cup Italian parsley, chopped

¼ cup olive oil

6 cloves garlic, smashed

1 egg

Marinara sauce for plating

Dice challah and ciabatta, and bake in 250-degree oven until dried. Process into fine crumbs in food processor.

Place prepared peppers in microwave-safe dish with ¼-inch water. Cover and microwave for 6–8 minutes.

Smash the garlic, and sauté in oil until slightly brown. Remove, and discard garlic. Brown sausage in the oil, breaking up into fine pieces. (I actually placed the cooked and cooled sausage into the food processor and pulsed it about 5 times to get the fine consistency.)

Combine the parsley, breadcrumbs, and Parmesan, and mix into the sausage. Add a little more oil if mixture is not a bit moist. Then add the egg, and mix thoroughly.

Stuff the peppers and arrange in a 3-quart casserole. Drizzle a bit of oil over all, and bake covered at 350 degrees for 45 minutes. Remove cover, and bake another 15 minutes.

Heat marinara sauce. Place about 2 tablespoons on plate; top with pepper, and enjoy!

UNSTUFFED CABBAGE

Michele Kaplan of Kansas City and I were talking recipes one evening at her mother, Pauline Hendel's home. She told me about this recipe, and after we went back and forth about the use of Ragu Italian sauce, she assured me it worked! I made a casserole, and to a person, everyone went back for seconds! I just tweaked it a tiny bit.

MEATBALLS:

2 pounds ground beef

1 teaspoon salt

2 eggs

½ teaspoon pepper

½ cup water

4 tablespoons raw rice

⅔ cup breadcrumbs or matzo meal

1 onion, large, chopped finely

SAUCE:

1 (16 ounce) can whole cranberry sauce

1 (12 ounce) jar chili sauce

1 (14 ounce) jar Ragu Italian sauce or any good marinara sauce

1 cup water

¼ cup brown sugar or to taste

2–3 tablespoons lemon juice or to taste

Salt to taste

1 medium cabbage, coarsely chopped

2 bay leaves

Combine all ingredients for meatballs, and mix well. Shape into a bit smaller than golf ball size, and place on cookie sheet to bake at 350 degrees for 15–20 minutes until lightly browned.

While meatballs are baking, combine first four sauce ingredients in saucepan and heat. Adjust sweet and sour balance with sugar and lemon juice. Add salt to taste.

In a large casserole dish, layer chopped cabbage, then the meatballs, and lastly pour sauce over all. Tuck in the bay leaves, and bake, uncovered, for 1 hour at 325 degrees. Gently stir; then cover, and bake for 2 more hours.

BARBARA HEIMANN

MISCELLANEOUS

DILL PICKLES

BEACH CLUB BREAD SPREAD

My visitors, especially my grandchildren, all love this spread that the club serves with lavosh crackers. I always embarrassingly have to ask for another basket.

Ranch dressing mix

Cream cheese

Garlic

Butter

Whip all together, and enjoy!

DILL PICKLES WITH HONEY AND JALAPEÑO

Lisa took me out for brunch at The Mercantile at Union Station in Denver. After brunch we walked around the shopping area, and I spotted a jar of pickle spears that looked so beautiful I just had to buy them!
As it turns out, they were perfect! Dilly, a bit sweet, and a tad hot. I looked at the ingredients and tried to make them with quite good results.

Makes 3 (1 quart) jars or a ½ gallon container

12 Kirby cucumbers, each cut into 4 spears

1 bunch dill

1–2 cloves garlic each jar

1½ tablespoons pickling spice each jar

2 jalapeños, cut in half vertically, each jar

1 medium onion, chunked and divided among jars

4 cups water

1½ cups white vinegar

1 cup wildflower honey (the Turkish Honey from Trader Joe's if you can get it)

½ teaspoon salt

Sprinkle red pepper flakes

Place garlic, pickling spice, and onion in bottom of each jar. Then stand cucumber spears and jalapeños upright in the jars. This is easier to do if you lay the jar on its side and begin to fill the jar that way; then stand it up and finish. Put some of the smaller spears horizontally on top of the vertical spears. Top off with the fresh dill. Set aside.

Bring water, vinegar, honey, salt, and pepper flakes to a boil. Then carefully pour the hot liquid over the prepared ingredients in each jar. Place lids on the jars, and let cool before refrigerating. Give them at least a day in the fridge, and then start munching!

MARINADE FOR POULTRY

As usual, Barbara Cohen has come up with a simple, yet delicious marinade for poultry!

Rub poultry with Dijon mustard.

Drizzle honey over all.

Pour Worcestershire sauce over all poultry, and bake!

MOROCCAN MATBUCHA

This is an excellent accompaniment to eggs, meat, chicken, or fish, especially if you like hot and spicy.

2 green peppers

1 jalapeño, seeded and finely diced

1 large can Italian plum tomatoes; seed tomatoes and save

½ juice from can

1 clove garlic, minced

2 teaspoons sugar

1 teaspoon chili flakes

½ teaspoon salt

⅓ cup olive oil

1 tablespoon paprika

Place green pepper in 400-degree oven until charred. Remove from oven, and place in bag or covered container to loosen skin. When cool, remove peel, seed, and chop.

Sauté garlic in oil briefly, and then add tomatoes, green peppers, and seasonings. Cook for four hours on low. Add tomato juice as needed; ½ hour before finishing, taste for seasoning, and add ½ jalapeño. Then add more jalapeño to adjust to taste. This lasts several weeks in refrigerator.

SWEET AND SOUR PEPPERS

Pauline Hendel, my nonagenarian friend who still entertains at home, served these at one of her dinner parties, and now I usually have some in the refrigerator for a healthy snack.

9 large peppers (multicolored)

4 cups water

1½ cups white vinegar

1 cup sugar or ½ cup Domino Light (sugar and Stevia blend)

Garlic to taste (2 or 3 cloves)

Red pepper flakes to taste

Place garlic and pepper flakes in bottom of 3 jars or 1 large canister jar.

Boil water, vinegar, and sugar.

Place cut peppers in canister, and pour hot mixture over to blanch peppers.

Seal hot, and refrigerate when cool.

Can use the next day. These last for several weeks in the fridge.

*I've done this recipe with a package of 6 multicolored peppers from Costco. I reduced all ingredients then to 3 cups water, 1 cup white vinegar, ¾ cup sugar, 2 large garlic cloves, and crushed pepper flakes to taste.

PASTA, GRAINS, AND RICE

GREEK PASTA SALAD

BRENDA'S DELICIOUS MAC AND CHEESE

My sister-in-law, Brenda Blatt, sent a request for help with a menu she was planning. This is one of the dishes she will serve. What could be better?

Kosher salt

Vegetable oil

16 ounces macaroni or Cavatappi noodles

4½ cups whole milk

8 tablespoons (1 stick) unsalted butter, divided

½ cup all-purpose flour

10 ounces extra-sharp cheddar, grated

10 ounces Gruyère, grated

½ teaspoon freshly ground pepper

1½ cups panko crumbs

Preheat oven to 375 degrees.

Drizzle oil into large pot of boiling water, salted. Add pasta, and cook as directed to al dente (will still cook when baking later) around 6 minutes.

Meanwhile, make a roux: heat the milk in a small saucepan, but don't boil.

Melt 6 tablespoons butter in a large pot, and add flour. Cook over low heat for 2 minutes, stirring with whisk. While whisking, add the hot milk, and cook for a minute or 2 more until thickened and smooth. Off the heat, add Gruyère, cheddar, 1 tablespoon salt, and pepper. Add the cooked pasta and stir well. Pour into a 3-quart baking dish. Prepare to this point, and refrigerate if doing a day before serving.

When ready to bake, bring macaroni to room temperature. Melt the remaining 2 tablespoons butter, and combine with panko. Sprinkle panko on top, and bake for 30–35 minutes or until the sauce is bubbly and the macaroni is browned on top.

BUTTERNUT SQUASH LASAGNA

While I was in Colorado, Stephanie had a taste for my won ton lasagna, which is made with marinara and spinach among other ingredients, especially mushrooms. It turns out Robin, Lisa's husband, doesn't like mushrooms—who knew? Since he was making the effort to take the bus up to Louisville from Denver after working all day, I decided to make lasagna that he might like. He liked it!

Serves 8

Wonton wraps—packages often found in produce section

WHITE SAUCE:

¼ cup butter

¼ cup flour

3½ cups milk

1 cup fresh basil, chiffonade (roll leaves together, and cut thinly crosswise)

Salt and pepper, pinch of nutmeg

16 ounces ricotta

1 egg

Oregano, basil, or if preferred—sage

1 large butternut squash peeled and chunked into 1-inch cubes, about 4 cups.

Mozzarella cheese about 2 cups or an Italian blend

Parmesan for topping

Sauté squash in a bit of olive oil until slightly browned, and then add about ½ cup water to pan. Cover, and simmer for 20 minutes, stirring every so often. Cool, then mash. Set aside.

For white sauce, melt the butter in a pot; then add the flour, and cook for about a minute together. Slowly add the milk while stirring so the flour is not lumpy. Cook sauce on a low heat until thickened. Add seasonings. Set aside.

Mix ricotta, egg, and herbs. Set aside.

To assemble lasagna:

Butter 9×13 inch Pyrex. Spread about ⅓ cup white sauce on bottom. Layer wonton wraps, 3 across and 4 down; spread squash over, dollop with ricotta, and then sprinkle mozzarella. Pour more white sauce on, and continue in same fashion twice more. Top with won ton and sprinkle just a little bit of mozzarella on top. Cover with aluminum foil, and bake at 375 degrees for 40 minutes. Uncover and sprinkle ⅓ cup Parmesan and a bit of mozzarella on top and return to oven for 15 minutes uncovered until nicely browned. Remove from oven, and let rest for 10–15 minutes.

COLUMBIAN RICE AND BEANS

Stephanie makes this, and it provides a healthy meal for her and anyone lucky enough to share the meal.

RICE:

1½ cups white or brown rice

3 cups water

½ bunch scallions, sliced

3 cloves garlic

2 tablespoons salt

1 tablespoon olive oil

1 lime, juiced

BEANS:

1 onion, chopped

½ bunch scallions, sliced

8 cloves garlic, minced

1 tablespoon salt

1 teaspoon sugar

2 cans black beans, undrained

1 (14½ ounce) can diced tomatoes with juice

Cilantro, handful (optional)

Cheddar, grated (optional)

Place all rice ingredients in pot, and cover. Cook until all liquid is absorbed. If using brown rice, you may have to add a bit more water toward the end of cooking.

In the meantime, sauté onion, garlic, and scallions in olive oil until onions are soft. Season with the salt and sugar. Add the beans and tomatoes, and simmer, uncovered, for ½ hour. Add the cilantro, if using, and simmer for ½ hour more.

Spoon the beans over the rice, and grate some cheddar over.

COUSCOUS WITH CHICKEN AND FETA

Lynni Mendelson made this for one of our bridge lunches—easily made with some ready-bought items. I keep the dressing on hand to use on a variety of salads.

1 (5½ ounce) box Near East Toasted Pine Nut Couscous

1¼ cups broth, can be chicken or veggie

2 teaspoons olive oil

3 cups cooked chicken, chopped

¼ cup basil, chopped

¼ pound feta cheese, crumbles

1 pint grape tomatoes, halved

DRESSING:

1 shallot, finely minced

1 teaspoon grainy Dijon mustard

¼ cup white balsamic vinegar

½ cup extra virgin olive oil

1 teaspoon salt

Pepper, freshly ground.

Mix dressing and set aside. Prepare couscous, using the broth and olive oil, according to directions on package. Then cool the couscous and fluff it. Add the chicken (can be from a bought rotisserie chicken), basil, feta, and tomatoes. Toss with some of the dressing. You won't need all of it. This can be served warm or at room temperature.

COUSCOUS WITH CHICKPEAS

As we Youngstowners so often do, we pitch together and make the most flavorful dinners. I took this couscous to a party for Paula Domsky's 80th, and it was served as an accompaniment to Chicken Marbella. I doubled the recipe with excellent results.

Serves 4–6

2 cups water

1½ cups Israeli pearl couscous (toasted)

¾ teaspoon kosher salt

1 (16 ounce) can chickpeas, rinsed, and drained

¼ cup pine nuts, toasted

½ cup chopped Italian parsley

½ scallion, finely chopped

4 ounces feta cheese, crumbled (optional)

Salt and pepper to taste

DRESSING:

3 tablespoons lemon juice

1 clove garlic, minced

⅓ cup extra virgin olive oil

Whisk all ingredients together and set aside.

Preheat oven to 300 degrees.

Bring water and salt to boil in medium saucepan. Add couscous and stir, and remove from heat. Cover, and let stand for 10 minutes.

Transfer the couscous to oven-proof dish, and fluff with a fork. Add just enough lemon dressing to season, and add chickpeas to the couscous. Bake the mixture in a 300-degree oven for 20–25 minutes. Fluff halfway through baking, and then remove from oven when couscous is dry and toasty.

Place couscous in a serving bowl and bring to room temperature. Add rest of lemon dressing; then toss in pine nuts, parsley, scallions and, if using, the feta. Adjust seasoning with salt and pepper. Serve at room temperature.

FRESH TOMATO BASIL EGG PASTA

JoAnn Roth put me onto this recipe in one of Ina Garten's books. Ina uses angel hair pasta, but JoAnn steered me to these wonderful German egg noodles, cut short and thin, which eliminate the messy slurpiness of spaghetti. I have successfully cut this recipe in half, and it actually served 6 as an ample side dish. When I serve this, I usually don't make a salad. A few days before I plan to make this recipe, I let my tomatoes ripen on the counter until ready to use. So sweet!

Serves 10

4 pints cherry tomatoes

½ cup extra virgin olive oil

4–6 cloves garlic, minced

20 large basil leaves plus more for garnish

Pinch of red pepper flakes or more if you like

Salt and pepper

17.6-ounce bag Bechtle Traditional German Egg Pasta

1½ cups Parmigiano reggiano, grated

About noon the day you plan on serving this for supper, place the oil, garlic, basil, crushed red pepper, and about ¾ teaspoon salt and freshly ground pepper in a bowl large enough to hold all other ingredients. Mix all these ingredients together, and then halve the tomatoes and just place them in the bowl on top of the olive oil mixture. Cover bowl with plastic wrap and set on counter until ready to finish dish. When ready to serve, bring a large pot of salted (1 tablespoon salt) water to boil. Put noodles in water and boil for exactly 2½ minutes. Drain and add to to-matoes in bowl. Mix the Parmigiano through, garnish with some more torn basil leaves, and serve to delighted diners!

*If you can't find the Bechtle noodles—in European section in my grocery store—they are available on Amazon.

*I also macerate the tomatoes as described and then throw them into a large salad of romaine and pesto chicken cut up and then add the parmesan. I then sprinkle just enough balsamic vinegar to balance the olive oil.

GREEK PASTA SALAD

JoAnn Roth saved my New Year's Day lunch when she gave me this recipe that she had served to raves over the Xmas holiday. It's a great dish to do ahead along with the slow-roasted salmon I had planned for the menu. The dressing is also terrific in a salad, substituting romaine for the pasta.

Serves 12

⅔ cup extra virgin olive oil

⅓ cup red wine vinegar

4 teaspoons fresh lemon juice

1⅓ tablespoons sugar

2 teaspoons dried parsley

2 teaspoons dried oregano leaves

1½ teaspoons finely minced fresh garlic

⅔ teaspoon table salt

⅔ teaspoon coarse ground black pepper

SALAD:

1 (16 ounce) package orecchiette pasta

1 (14.5 ounce) can garbanzo beans, drained and rinsed

⅓ cup finely chopped red onion

7 ounces feta cheese, cubed or crumbled

1 (9.5 ounce) jar sliced Kalamata olives, drained

1¼ cups artichoke hearts marinated in oil, halves and quarters, chop them if too big

3 cups chopped Persian cucumbers or English cucumbers

30 grape tomatoes, sliced lengthwise

⅛ cup fresh oregano leaves

For the dressing, add all ingredients to a pint-sized jar and shake until fully combined. Let dressing sit for at least 2 hours so the flavors meld. The dressing can easily be made up to two days in advance and kept in the refrigerator.

Cook the pasta in salted water according to package directions. Drain, and rinse well, making sure the pasta is cooled down and the shells aren't sticking together.

When the pasta has cooled, transfer it to a large bowl and toss it with ¼ of the dressing until fully combined. Add the garbanzo beans, red onion, feta cheese, olives, artichoke hearts, and oregano leaves. Toss together with the pasta.

Cover the bowl with plastic wrap, and refrigerate for at least four hours or up to 24 hours. When ready to serve, add the cucumbers, tomato, and fresh oregano, and then toss with more dressing to your liking.

MATZO LASAGNA

Noah and Ilene were in charge of lunch one Passover day, and they made this delicious lasagna. It really takes no time, bakes quickly, and is impressive. When I reproduced the recipe for friends, the 3-quart casserole of lasagna was pretty much eaten by seven of us, with the exception of three small pieces.

Serves 8

6 matzo boards (I prefer Yehuda brand)

Salted water for soaking matzos

1 container (15–16 ounces) ricotta cheese

8 ounces cottage cheese, can be 2%

1 egg

Garlic, 1 clove, minced, or 1 cube Dorot crushed garlic*

Basil, several leaves shredded finely, or 1 cube Dorot chopped basil (Dorot Herbs found in frozen-food section)*

Marinara sauce (24–26 ounce jar)

6 ounces fresh baby spinach

4 ounces shredded mozzarella cheese

¼ cup Parmesan, grated

Preheat oven to 350 degrees.

Mix ricotta, cottage cheese, the egg, garlic, and basil in a small bowl; set aside.

Spread a thin layer of marinara sauce over the bottom of a 9×13 inch baking dish.

Soak 2 matzos in warm salted water just until they're pliable—not too wet!

Layer the matzos over the sauce. You will have to break one of them and fill in spaces to fit.

Tear up ⅓ of spinach over the matzos. Dollop ⅓ of the cheese mixture over the spinach. Spread ⅓ of remaining marinara over cheese. Sprinkle with a bit of the Parmesan.

Continue in this manner two more times with two matzos for each layer, and top with the shredded mozzarella.

Bake in 350-degree oven for ½ hour or until top is nicely browned. *You may use garlic powder and dried basil.

PENNE WITH ROASTED VEGETABLES

Serves 6–8

2 red bell peppers

2 poblano peppers

2 ears corn

8 ounces penne pasta

2 cups grape tomatoes halved

½ cup onion, finely chopped

¼ cup chopped parsley or cilantro

1 cup avocado, chopped

¾ cup queso fresco

DRESSING:

2 tablespoons lime juice

1 tablespoon olive oil

1 teaspoon salt

½ teaspoon pepper

½ teaspoon cumin

1 clove garlic, minced

Cut all peppers in half, and remove all seeds and membranes. Rub olive oil over peppers and corn, and place on baking sheet. Bake at 400 degrees until skins are turning black and corn is charred, about 20 minutes. When done place peppers in Ziploc bag for about 10 minutes; then skins will slip off easily.

Shuck corn and coarsely chop peppers.

Cook pasta in salted water until al dente.

Mix all dressing ingredients.

When pasta and roasted vegetables are room temperature, mix with the tomatoes, onions, parsley, and avocado.

Add dressing and sprinkle queso fresco over top.

*If preparing ahead, don't add avocado and cheese until just before serving.

SPANAKOPITA LASAGNA

I like to make lasagna because it freezes well. This recipe calls for an 8-inch square dish. It easily doubles for a 3- or 4-quart casserole.

Serves 4–6

BÉCHAMEL:

2 tablespoons butter

2 tablespoons flour

2 cups milk

¼ teaspoon salt

Pepper, freshly ground

Pinch of nutmeg

LASAGNA:

Wonton wrappers

1 teaspoon olive oil

¼ red onion, chopped

3 scallions, thinly sliced

1 clove garlic, minced

1 (16 ounce) package frozen chopped spinach, thawed, and drained

¼ cup Italian parsley, chopped

¼ pound feta cheese—Balkan style "Pastures of Eden" from Trader Joe's or Greek feta crumbled

¼ cup parmesan, grated

1 egg

¼ cup dill, chopped

½ teaspoon mint, dried

½ teaspoon oregano, dried

*Extra parmesan for topping

Preheat oven to 350 degrees.

Prepare béchamel. Melt the butter in a saucepan, add the flour, and stir for about a minute. Slowly add the milk, and simmer for 10 minutes. Add the salt, pepper, and nutmeg, and stir. Set aside.

Sauté the onion, scallions, and garlic in the oil until wilted. Add the thawed and drained spinach, and continue cooking for about 5 minutes. Then add the parsley, and mix through. Set aside.

In a separate bowl, combine the feta, parmesan, egg, dill, mint, and oregano. Mix until the egg is thoroughly incorporated.

To assemble:

Pour béchamel into the bottom of the casserole dish just to cover.

Top with the wonton wrappers, overlapping them a bit.

Spread ⅓ of the spinach mixture over, and then dollop ⅓ of the feta mixture over that.

Again, pour some béchamel over; top with wontons, and continue in the same way two more times. Top the last layer of feta with won tons in a decorative pattern. Finish with the rest of the béchamel, and sprinkle some parmesan over all. Place in oven, and bake for 40 minutes.

WILD RICE, APRICOT, AND BREAD DRESSING

This has been a hit twice now at family Thanksgivings, so I think it will just have to be a regular on future holiday menus. It doesn't seem quite as heavy as traditional stuffing. It can be prepared one or two days ahead, then baked before serving.

Serves 10–12

½ –¾ cup wild rice

1 cup chopped walnuts, pecans, or slivered almonds, toasted

1 cup chestnuts (if no chestnuts, just add 1 more cup of the above nuts)

1½ cups chopped celery

1 onion, chopped

⅓ cup butter or margarine

1 cup long grain white or brown rice

3 cups vegetable or chicken broth

1 cup apricot nectar

½ cup brandy (optional)—if not adding, replace amount with broth or nectar

2 teaspoons dried thyme

1 teaspoon rubbed sage

½ teaspoon ground nutmeg

Salt and pepper

6 cups (8 ounces) herbed bread-cube stuffing

1 cup dried apricots, small dice

2 tablespoons chopped parsley (optional)

Bring 6 cups water to a boil in a small saucepan. Add rinsed, drained wild rice to boiling water. Return to boil and reduce heat; cover, and simmer until rice begins to split, about 45 minutes. Drain.

In a large sauté pan, stir celery and onion in melted butter, and cook until onion is limp—10 minutes. Add white or brown rice and stir until all rice is well coated, 3 minutes. Add broth, nectar, brandy, and spices. Bring to a boil, reduce heat, and cover. Cook until rice is tender to the bite.

Stir in bread cubes, apricots, and wild rice, and stir until bread is evenly moist. Pour into greased 3-quart casserole and cover tightly. Can cool and refrigerate at this point or bake at 350 degrees for 30 to 40 minutes. Uncover top for last 15 minutes. Sprinkle with parsley, and serve.

POULTRY

CHICKEN WITH FIGS READY FOR THE OVEN

BARBARA HEIMANN

ALBANIAN GRILLED CHICKEN

I love the chicken keparo at Pelago's Restaurant in Naples. This may be a close facsimile. The chicken is very good served over your favorite rice recipe or simply sliced down and served in pita with tzatziki sauce. If serving in pita, omit topping.

Serves 4–6

CHICKEN:

4 lemons, 2 zested and juiced, and 2 halved

¼ cup Dijon mustard

2 tablespoons finely chopped rosemary leaves

1 teaspoon crushed red pepper flakes

6 boneless, skinless chicken breast halves, sliced in half horizontally

Kosher salt

TOPPING:

Green olives, pitted and sliced

Greek olives, pitted and sliced

Baby tomatoes, halved

Seedless red grapes, halved

Combine the lemon juice, zest, mustard, rosemary, and crushed red pepper in a small bowl. Add 1–2 tablespoons of olive oil to the mustard mixture to loosen it. Paint this mixture generously all over the chicken, and let sit for up to 2 hours at room temperature or overnight in the refrigerator. If you have any of the mustard mixture left over, save it for repainting while the chicken is cooking.

Bring chicken to room temperature. Prepare mixture of topping for chicken — mixing all ingredients equally except for the olives; put a bit less of them in the mix.

Place chicken and lemon halves, cut side down, on the grill. Do not disturb the lemons until they look brown and caramelized. They will smell great while they are cooking too! The chicken will cook quickly, and both lemons and chicken should be done at the same time.

Remove the chicken from the grill to a serving platter. Top with the tomato mixture, and serve with the grilled lemon halves. Squeeze the grilled lemon over the chicken before eating for extra lemony goodness.

CHICKEN WITH FIGS

About the time I was seeing fresh figs in the markets, I started finding recipes in the newspapers and magazines featuring them. As it happened, the New York Times ran an article by Melissa Clark about using figs in a Rosh Hashanah chicken recipe. Oddly enough that same day I went to a new restaurant in Naples — Mediterrano, owned by a Syrian man, and guess what was on the menu? Right - chicken and figs! And yes, I ordered it. Their version was good, but I decided to combine ideas from both sources and came up with this recipe. I had friends over to test the results, and we all would definitely like this meal again.

Serves 6

Marinate one day ahead

4 pounds chicken breast halves, skin on, bone in (each about 1 pound, then cut in half horizontally) or any combination of chicken pieces preferred

1 tablespoon salt

2 sprigs rosemary

2–3 cloves garlic, minced

1 navel orange

1 pound fresh figs

1 jalapeño, seeded and cut into strips (optional)

1 red onion, in ⅓-inch slices

1–2 shallots

10 mini peppers, stem end cut and seeds removed

Handful of apricots

1 lemon

Olive oil

Prepare chicken for marinating. Salt the chicken. Mince the garlic on a micro plane, and rub over the chicken pieces; then grate the orange on the micro plane until you get about a tablespoon of zest, and rub that into the chicken. Save the orange for using in the final preparation. Strip the rosemary stems; rub the rosemary into the breasts, and marinate overnight.

Preheat oven to 450 degrees. Place chicken pieces in pan large enough so there is plenty of room around them. Remove stems from figs, and cut in half. Scatter in pan. Do the same with the sliced onions, shallots, mini peppers, and apricots. Finally slice the orange, and cut each slice in half. Nestle the orange among the chicken and other ingredients in pan. Throw on the jalapeño strips. Quarter a lemon and slightly drizzle a bit of lemon juice over the chicken, and place the lemon in the pan as well. Drizzle olive oil over the entire preparation.

Bake for ½ hour. Baste with the juices. Can remove from oven at this point if need time before serving. Kick oven up to 475 degrees, and finish the chicken so the skin is nice and brown, about another 10–15 minutes.

*I use a convection oven—temperatures for that are 425 and 450 degrees.

**I served the chicken with a barley, wild rice, and cranberry mixture alongside.

CHICKEN PROVENÇAL

Some recipes are iconic, and I believe this from the New York Times is one of them. I've served it to family and as a dinner party dish for friends. The savory aroma emanating from the oven is a wonderful hint of the memorable meal to come!

8 bone-in, skin-on chicken thighs, trimmed of fat and excess skin, or chicken breasts, skin-on, cut into half cross-wise, or combination

2 teaspoons kosher salt

1 teaspoon freshly ground black pepper

½–¾ cup all-purpose flour

3 tablespoons olive oil

2 tablespoons herbes de Provence

1 lemon, quartered

8–10 cloves garlic, peeled

4–6 medium-size shallots, peeled and halved

⅓ cup dry vermouth

4 sprigs of thyme, for serving

Preheat oven to 400 degrees. Swirl the oil in a large roasting pan.

Season the chicken with salt and pepper. Put the flour in a shallow pan, and lightly dredge the chicken in it, shaking the pieces to remove excess flour.

Place the floured chicken in oiled roasting pan. Season the chicken with the herbes de Provence. Arrange the lemons, garlic cloves, and shallots around the chicken, and then add the vermouth to the pan.

Put the pan in the oven, and roast for 25–30 minutes; then baste it with the pan juices. Continue roasting for an additional 25–30 minutes or until the chicken is very crisp and the meat is cooked through. Serve on platter, garnished with thyme.

CUBANELLE PEPPERS STUFFED WITH TURKEY AND CORN

I like vegetables stuffed; they're wonderful for a buffet — 1 or 2 peppers, one serving! I got the idea for the turkey from an Ottolenghi cookbook. They make the ground turkey mixture into meatballs and sauté them; then serve with a roasted pepper sauce.

⅔ cup corn kernels fresh, or frozen roasted corn (available at Trader Joe's)

½ cup breadcrumbs

1 pound ground turkey breast

1 egg

4 green onions, finely chopped

2 tablespoons Italian parsley, finely chopped

2½ teaspoons cumin

1½ teaspoon salt

½ teaspoon black pepper

1 clove garlic, minced

Cubanelle peppers, halved, and seeded

If using fresh corn, toss into a hot nonstick pan for a few minutes until it has a slight char. Add the corn to the rest of the ingredients and mix by hand. Don't overwork the mixture. Pour mixture into the pepper halves and arrange on a parchment-lined pan. Bake at 350 degrees until done. Place stuffed peppers on serving platter with red pepper sauce alongside, or drizzle some of the sauce over.

ROASTED PEPPER SAUCE

4 red bell peppers

3 tablespoons olive oil

1 teaspoon salt

Small handful Italian parsley

1 clove garlic, minced

1 small mild chili, seeded

2 tablespoons sweet chili sauce

2 tablespoons cider vinegar

Preheat oven to 400 degrees.

Quarter and seed the peppers. Shave off all the white parts. Toss with 2 table-spoons of the olive oil and ½ teaspoon salt. Place in baking pan, and bake for 35 minutes until soft. Transfer to a bowl, and cover with plastic wrap. Once they have cooled, you can easily peel the skin off. And then place the peppers in a food processor with their roasting juices, and add the rest of the sauce ingredients. Process until smooth and adjust seasonings. Set aside until ready to use.

GRILLED CHICKEN

This is the best! I like to have these leftover in the fridge for sandwiches.

4 pounds chicken breasts, boneless

MARINADE:

4 lemons, zested

Juice from 1 lemon

Honey mustard

Olive oil

Basil

Salt, pepper

Mix marinade.

Slice breasts in half horizontally,

Slather breasts with marinade, and refrigerate for a few hours.

Grill until done. Because these are thinner pieces of chicken, they will cook quickly. Keep an eye on them.

GRILLED ROSEMARY CHICKEN WITH CORN QUINOA

This can be served at room temperature for a light lunch or easy summer dinner.

4 chicken breasts, boneless, skinless

Salt, pepper

Rosemary

Olive oil

QUINOA:

1¼ cup red quinoa cooked in four cups water and ½ teaspoon salt

4 shallots, thinly sliced

2 cloves garlic, minced

2 cups fresh corn kernels

6 cups shard or any greens of your choice

½ cup torn basil

¼ cup torn mint

2 tablespoons lemon juice

Rub chicken breasts with a bit of oil, and season with salt and pepper. Sprinkle rosemary over, and marinate a few hours before grilling.

Sauté shallots until soft, and add garlic. Sauté a bit more, and then add fresh corn.

Stir all together and add shard, and cook until just wilted. Drain quinoa, and add to vegetables. When ready to serve, add the basil, mint, and lemon juice.

Place some quinoa on dinner plate, and top with some slices of the grilled chicken.

ORANGE CHICKEN

I found this in my late sister-in-law Marilyn Stein's recipe box, and she had named it "Barbara's Chicken". What goes around comes around.

6 chicken breasts, bone-in, skinned

SAUCE:

1 (6 ounce) can frozen orange juice

¼ cup butter, melted

1 teaspoon ground ginger

¼ cups soy sauce

2 teaspoons curry powder

1 tablespoon dry mustard

GARNISH:

1 avocado, sliced (optional)

1 (8 ounce) can pineapples chunks, drained

½ cup slivered almonds, toasted

Preheat oven to 350 degrees.

Combine orange juice, butter, ginger, soy sauce, curry powder, and mustard. Place chicken in baking pan with orange juice sauce and marinate up to one hour. Then place in oven and bake for one hour, or until done, at 350 degrees. Baste as chicken is cooking. Serve over rice with garnishes.

STUFFING FOR TURKEY

My grandson, Jake, loves chestnuts so we tend to go overboard on them, and add more than the recipe calls for. Also, veggie broth can be used, and then this is a satisfying vegetarian dish!

1 loaf challah, cubed and toasted

1 package Pepperidge Farm Herb Stuffing cubes

2–3 tablespoons vegetable oil

1–2 onions, diced

2 stalks celery, diced

1 carrot, shredded or small dice

1 pound mushrooms, sliced and chopped

Chicken broth, or boiling water mixed with Osem powder to make broth

2 eggs

Salt to taste

Pepper to taste

Poultry seasoning, if needed

1 cup roasted chestnuts or ⅓ cup toasted pine nuts, optional

Butter or margarine for top of stuffing.

*This is an approximate recipe—nothing is exact because the amount of broth depends on how much liquid is absorbed, and the seasonings and vegetables can be varied according to taste.

Prepare challah—can do ahead of time.

Heat oil in large pan, and sauté onions, celery, and carrots until soft, about 10 minutes. Add mushrooms, and sauté 5 more minutes. Mix in the challah cubes and Pepperidge cubes. Add enough chicken broth to moisten all the bread. Beat eggs with a bit of water, and add to the stuffing mixture. Season to taste. Add chestnuts, if using, or pine nuts. If the consistency is not moist—you should be able to see the shape of the cubes, but they should be soft—add more broth as needed. Place all in greased 4-quart casserole. This can be done day before up to this point. When ready to use, bring to room temperature. Dot top with butter or margarine, and bake at 350 degrees for one hour. Cover with foil for first ½ hour; then uncover for another ½ hour until top is toasty.

TURKEY BREAST

Kathy and Bruce introduced me to this very easy way to make a turkey breast which 'hits the spot" when Alex and Cody come home for dinner after an energetic day at work. Just marinate the turkey in the vinaigrette for several hours or overnight, and roast until done.

*After you marinate the turkey, remove the breast to a roasting pan, and refrigerate for a few hours to dry out the skin a bit. The skin will be crispier then when done.

TURKEY:

3 pounds turkey breast, bone in

Gerard Champagne Vinaigrette

Preheat oven to 400 degrees.

Marinate the turkey breast in vinaigrette, preferably overnight. Remove from marinade, and pat dry. If you have time, refrigerate for a bit; then bring back to room temperature and roast until internal temperature is 165 degrees.

Another way:

TURKEY BREAST—BROWN SUGAR RUBBED:

3 pounds turkey breast

2 tablespoons brown sugar

1 teaspoon parsley flakes

1 teaspoon paprika

½ teaspoon each—garlic powder, onion powder, salt, dry mustard

¼ teaspoon each—cinnamon, pepper, ginger

Preheat oven to 400 degrees.

Combine all seasoning ingredients, and rub all over turkey breast; can be done evening before. Bring seasoned turkey to room temperature. Bake for 1 hour or until internal temperature is 165 degrees.

TURKEY, MARINATED AND GRILLED

This recipe comes from Linda Sniderman. She and Howard highly recommend it! Note Linda's method of cooking this in the oven, which she does during the cold winter months in Youngstown.

Serves 8

MARINADE:

1 cup brown sugar

4 cloves garlic, minced

2 tablespoons minced fresh ginger root

1½ tablespoons poppy seeds

2 scallions minced

1½ cups soy sauce

¼ cup extra virgin olive oil

2 tablespoons rice wine vinegar

Juice of 3 lemons

⅛ teaspoon freshly ground black pepper

4 or more pounds turkey breast, de-boned with skin on

GLAZE:

½ cup apricot preserves

¼ cup Dijon mustard or wasabi mustard

1 tablespoon minced fresh ginger

In large bowl, whisk together the marinade ingredients. Pound turkey breast so the thickness is more even, and then add turkey to the marinade; turn to coat well. Marinate, covered, overnight or up to two days.

Preheat grill. Remove turkey from marinade and pat dry.

Prepare glaze in a saucepan by heating on low until all is melted. Keep warm.

Grill turkey on each side for 15–20 minutes until turkey loses its pinkness inside.

Grill each side an additional 5 minutes after brushing it with the warm glaze. Allow turkey to stand 10 minutes before carving.

This freezes well once sliced. Reheat in microwave on medium power.

*To cook in oven: With skin add 1 inch of marinade to pan. Without skin add 1 inch of marinade and ¼ to ½ cup chicken broth to pan. Roast at 450- degrees uncovered on third rung up for 15 minutes. Turn down to 400 degrees for another 15 minutes, basting as it cooks. Then cover, and cook at 350 degrees for ½ hour, turning and basting twice.

BARBARA HEIMANN

SALAD

R1 SALAD

ARUGULA SALAD

Gloria makes a salad that has been making my family happy lately. You can just use the ingredients as you see fit. I actually slice the fennel and the red cabbage very thinly with the slicer blade on my Cuisinart, but a mandoline would do as well. Use proportions of the following as you like. However, use lots of arugula as that's the greens base of the salad.

Arugula

Fennel, very thinly sliced

Red cabbage, very thinly sliced

Orange

Avocado

Almonds, slivered

Basil, fresh

Feta, just a touch

For the dressing, just whisk some olive oil (twice as much as lemon juice and vinegar combined), lemon juice, a splash of balsamic vinegar, salt and pepper, and a sprinkle of Truvia.

BARBARA HEIMANN

APPLE SALAD WITH ARUGULA AND AVOCADO

I call this the 3 A's salad. And it gets an A+ for easy. It has a hint of autumn in it, so when the seasons change, bring it on!

3 cups shredded romaine

3 cups arugula

1 apple, diced

1 avocado, diced

¼ cup dried cranberries

¼ cup corn, can be fresh or frozen

¼ cup slivered almonds, toasted

¼ cup Parmesan cheese for topping

DRESSING:

¼ cup balsamic vinegar

1 tablespoon maple syrup

1 tablespoon Dijon mustard

¼ cup vegetable oil

Salt and pepper to taste

Prepare dressing by whisking all ingredients together and set aside. Place all salad ingredients in a large salad bowl, and toss with as much dressing as you like; you won't need it all. Sprinkle the Parmesan over all, and serve.

ARTICHOKE-FENNEL-ARUGULA SALAD

WSJ November 3, 2012. Eric Rupert's recipe. This is such a simple salad, yet sophisticated and light enough as a meal starter.

VINAIGRETTE:

1 small shallot, minced

3 tablespoons sherry vinegar

3 tablespoons olive oil

2 tablespoons canola oil

Sea salt

Freshly ground pepper

1 cup fennel, in ⅛-inch slices

½ lemon, juiced

12–16 frozen artichoke quarters, defrosted

8 cups arugula

3 ounces Parmesan, shaved thinly plus some extra for garnish

Let minced shallot sit in vinegar for 10 minutes. Then whisk in oils and season with salt and pepper. Sprinkle fennel with a bit of salt and lemon juice, and set aside for 5–10 minutes. In a large bowl, toss arugula with a pinch of salt, and gently toss the fennel, artichokes, and Parmesan with the arugula. Add half the vinaigrette and toss. Season with salt and pepper and then add more vinaigrette if needed. Garnish with extra Parmesan.

BEAN/CABBAGE SALAD WITH ONION VINAIGRETTE

SALAD:

1 (15 ounce) can black beans, rinsed, and drained

1 (15 ounce) can corn, drained

1 cup frozen peas

1 large red pepper, diced

½ small red cabbage, diced

VINAIGRETTE:

1 Vidalia onion

½ cup vegetable oil

¼ cup red wine vinegar

2 tablespoons sugar

1–2 tablespoons poppy seeds

Salt and pepper

Chunk onion and place in blender with oil, vinegar, and sugar. Blend until onion is emulsified. Add poppy seeds, salt, and pepper to your taste.

Mix all salad ingredients together, and dress with onion vinaigrette.

BRUSSELS SPROUTS SLAW

This recipe comes from Martha Stewart's Living Magazine. They come up with some excellent recipes.

Serves 6 – 8

1 pound Brussels sprouts, shredded

1 tablespoon lemon juice

¼ cup olive oil

1 cup hazelnut crunch (recipe follows)

Salt and pepper to taste

HAZELNUT CRUNCH:

¼ cup plus 1 tablespoon olive oil

¼ cup fresh rosemary leaves

2 tablespoons julienned lemon zest

1 cup hazelnuts (5 ounces), coarsely chopped

2 tablespoons sugar

2 tablespoons lemon juice

Salt and pepper to taste

Toss together the sprouts, juice, oil and ¾ cup of the nut crunch. Season with salt and pepper. Serve immediately with a garnish of the remaining crunch sprinkled on top.

Heat oil on medium-high heat and add rosemary and lemon zest to cook until fragrant—30 seconds or a bit more. Add hazelnuts and cook, stirring, until nuts are golden brown and zest and rosemary are crisp, 1 to 2 minutes more.

Add sugar and lemon juice and continue cooking and stirring just until nuts begin to caramelize. Season with salt and pepper and transfer to a bowl to cool completely.

Break apart into small pieces. The crunch can be made ahead and stored for a few days in an airtight container. The hazelnut crunch is easily doubled to serve as a topping for other salads or vegetables.

❧

BULGARIAN RED PEPPER SALAD

This recipe is adapted from the cookbook Zahav.

¼ cup olive oil

1 large Vidalia onion, chopped

1 tablespoon paprika

1 tablespoon red wine vinegar

4 red peppers, chopped

2 carrots, grated

½ cup Italian parsley, chopped

1 tablespoon sugar

¼ teaspoon salt

1 cup white beans, canned Northern, drained and rinsed

2 tablespoons chives, chopped

Sauté onions in oil about 10 minutes until softened, but not browned. Add paprika and stir for 1 minute. Add the vinegar and red peppers, and cook until peppers are very tender, about 10 minutes or so. Add the carrots, parsley, sugar, and salt and stir to combine.

Transfer the pepper mixture to a food processor and pulse until coarsely chopped. Remove to dish and stir in the white beans. Garnish with chives. Serve warm or at room temperature. Can make ahead and refrigerate for a few days.

CHICKEN SALAD WITH VIDALIA ONION DRESSING

This is a good do-ahead salad. I always dress salads lightly and as it turned out, this flavorful dressing went a long way.

2 large boneless chicken breasts, cooked and sliced or diced

3–4 ounces Maytag Bleu cheese, crumbled

3 heads hearts of romaine, chopped

1 bag prepared romaine lettuce salad

¼ cup finely diced red onion (optional)

½ apple, skin on, julienned (Honeycrisp)

1 medium avocado

Lemon juice

¼ cup pistachios

¼ cup dried cranberries

Braswell's Creamy Vidalia Onion Salad Dressing

(or make recipe for onion vinaigrette in Bean/Cabbage Salad recipe)

Since I always like to prepare ahead, in the morning, I sliced the lettuce into my salad spinner, added the bag of pre-washed romaine salad, washed the mix, and spun it dry. I then placed this into the serving bowl with the onion mixed through and topped with the apple, which I had drizzled with some lemon juice to keep from discoloring. I then placed two peeled halves of the avocado over that, and again drizzled lemon juice over; then covered with plastic wrap and put into the fridge until lunchtime.

When ready to serve, dice the avocado and toss lettuces in bowl with some of the salad dressing; then add the diced chicken and the blue cheese. Toss again, and add more dressing if needed. Finally, mix in the pistachios and cranberries.

❧

CUCUMBER, PISTACHIO, AND YOGURT SALAD

I adapted this recipe from a WSJ article—"Eat Istanbul" by Andy Harris.

Serves 4

6 Persian cucumbers cut into thin 3-inch spears

3 tablespoons unsalted pistachios, roughly chopped

3 tablespoons fresh mint

Salt and pepper to taste

DRESSING:

3 tablespoons pomegranate molasses

⅓ cup yogurt

2 tablespoons olive oil

Whisk dressing ingredients together. Combine salad ingredients in a bowl and toss the dressing in.

FARMERS' MARKET SALAD

When these vegetables were crisp in the heart of the summer, my mother made this simple salad for Dad, who loved it.

Kirby cucumbers (often used for making dill pickles), peeled

Red radishes

Scallions

Dill

Sour cream

Salt

Simply rough chop the vegetables in the proportion and amount needed for the number of people you want to serve. Figure 1½ cucumbers per person and go from there. Mix sour cream through the vegetables, add salt to taste, and serve.

FENNEL-HONEY SALAD

Corky Kaplan made this for lunch before one of our weekly mahjong games.

½ cup feta cheese, cubed

½ fennel bulb, thinly sliced

1 lemon, zested and juiced

¼ teaspoon kosher salt

¼ teaspoon pepper

2 tablespoons canola oil

6 ounces baby arugula (also called rocket)

2 tablespoons honey

Grape tomatoes and pine nuts, optional

Whisk lemon juice, zest, salt, pepper, honey, and oil until blended. Add fennel and toss. Let stand a few minutes to marinate. Place in bowl with the arugula and feta. Toss all together, and serve.

GARBANZO BEAN SALAD

On Shabbat, after the blessings, we often serve a fish appetizer and hummus or Middle Eastern-style salads to enjoy with the warm challah. This recipe wraps the flavors we like into one salad.

Serves 6–8

2 (15 ounce) cans garbanzo beans

1½ teaspoons black pepper, freshly ground

2 cloves garlic, smashed and peeled

3 tablespoons kosher salt, or more to taste

2 fresh thyme sprigs, or 1 teaspoon dried

1 fennel bulb, trimmed, cut in half, cored and thinly sliced (about 4 cups)

1 red onion, cut in half and thinly sliced (about 3 cups)

½ cup finely chopped fresh Italian parsley

DRESSING:

¾ teaspoon Dijon mustard

1 teaspoon smoked paprika

2 tablespoons fresh lemon juice

1 tablespoon white wine vinegar

½ cup extra virgin olive oil

Place the contents of the two cans of beans in a saucepan, and add 1 cup water, the garlic, 1 teaspoon pepper, and 1 teaspoon dried thyme. Bring to a boil, and immediately remove from heat, cover, and let stand for 15 minutes.

Meanwhile, in a small bowl, whisk together the Dijon mustard, the remaining ½ teaspoon pepper, the smoked paprika, lemon juice, and vinegar. Whisking constantly, slowly add the oil. Add salt to taste if necessary.

In a large bowl, toss the fennel and red onion with 3 tablespoons of the vinaigrette. Drain the beans, and discard the garlic. Toss the warm beans with the fennel and onion—the heat from the beans will soften the vegetables slightly. Cover with plastic wrap for about 15 minutes, and then stir in the remaining vinaigrette and toss with the parsley. (The salad can be made up to 1 day ahead, covered and refrigerated.) Serve warm or at room temperature.

GAZPACHO SHRIMP SALAD

1½ pounds peeled, de-veined frozen jumbo shrimp, uncooked

5 large ripe tomatoes

1 medium green pepper, chopped

1 medium red onion, chopped

1 English cucumber, chopped

2 cups good croutons

Italian parsley

1 recipe red pepper tomato dressing, below

DRESSING:

1 (12 ounce) jar roasted red peppers, drained

2 tomatoes, quartered

⅓ cup olive oil

2–3 tablespoons sherry vinegar

1 clove garlic

1 teaspoon smoked paprika

Thaw shrimp. Fill large skillet ½ full with salted water and a few bay leaves, and bring to boiling. Add shrimp. Cook uncovered for 1 minute. Remove skillet from heat, and let shrimp sit in water for 1–2 minutes until opaque. Remove with slotted spoon, discard bay leaves, and set aside to cool.

Dressing: Drain peppers. Blend with tomatoes, green pepper, onion, cucumber, and 2 tablespoons vinegar. Season with salt, pepper, and rest of vinegar if needed. Divide dressing among 6 bowls. Top with veggies, shrimp, croutons, and parsley.

BARBARA HEIMANN

GREEN GODDESS SALAD

When I was visiting Jana and Phoebe, I had this salad at the Goddess and Grocer in Chicago — I could eat it every day. It's billed as vegan because of the dressing, and if you leave out the blue cheese, it surely is!

Romaine

Red and yellow pepper, rough chop

Hard-boiled egg

Avocado

Tomato

Blue cheese, crumbled

Corn

Cucumber, diced

Chickpeas, rinsed, and drained

Carrot

GREEN GODDESS DRESSING:

⅓ cup tahini

½ cup apple cider vinegar

¼ cup soy sauce

2–3 tablespoons lemon juice

1–2 cloves garlic, minced

1 teaspoon sesame seeds, toasted

1 tablespoon parsley, chopped

1 tablespoon honey

1 teaspoon Dijon mustard

1 cup vegetable oil

Mix all the ingredients for the dressing, and starting with a bed of chopped romaine, just add all the other ingredients—as much or as little as suits you.

QUINOA CHOP-CHOP SALAD

I often eat at Farmhouse Kitchen in Boca, where members of my family and I always seem to gravitate to this—a salad. I have had it many times, and each time there are some different ingredients. So this is definitely one to experiment with. I don't believe you can go wrong as long as all the diced ingredients are approximately the same size and somewhat equal in quantity with the exception of the greens, perhaps a bit more of them.

1 cup red quinoa cooked in 2 cups salted water

½ cup French lentils, cooked according to package directions and cooled

½ pound green beans, blanched and cooled

Mixed greens—arugula, radicchio, chopped

1 carrot, small dice

1 stalk celery, small dice

1 ear corn, kernels removed from cob

¼ Fennel bulb, very thinly sliced

Craisins or golden raisins

Feta cheese or smoked Gouda

Almonds, or hazel nuts, toasted and finely chopped

OPTIONAL ADDITIONS:

Red onion, finely diced

1 pear, diced

Jicama, small dice

Avocado

DRESSING:

¼ cup cider vinegar

1–2 tablespoons Dijon

1–2 tablespoons honey or sugar to taste

½ cup vegetable oil

1 clove garlic

Basil

Thyme

Salt and pepper

Combine all ingredients for dressing, and emulsify in processor.

Prepare lentils and quinoa. Blanch green beans. Slice beans into ½-inch pieces.

Chop carrot and celery into small dice. Add rest of ingredients to your liking. Ingredients should be roughly the same size. Dress lightly. Only use enough greens and avocado for use at time of serving. Otherwise salad is good for a few days in fridge.

QUINOA AND KALE WITH GRILLED CHICKEN

This is another of Gary Murphy's recipes from the Naples Ritz Carlton.

Serves 4

1 cup quinoa

2 cups water

1 teaspoon garlic powder

Salt and pepper to taste

SALAD:

1 package baby kale

1 pint baby heirloom tomatoes

½ cup toasted pumpkin seeds

8 ounces goat cheese or feta

4 grilled chicken breasts, sliced

VINAIGRETTE:

½ cup red wine vinegar

1½ teaspoons Dijon mustard

1 tablespoon catsup

1½ tablespoons honey

1¼ cups vegetable oil

1 clove garlic, minced

Salt and pepper to taste

Prepare quinoa by placing the quinoa, water, and seasonings in a saucepan and bringing to a boil. Reduce heat; cover, and simmer until all liquid is gone, about 15 minutes. Fluff quinoa and cool.

Place all the kale and tomatoes in a salad bowl along with the cooled quinoa. Toss with some of the vinaigrette. Add the pumpkin seeds, cheese, and chicken and toss once more. Add more dressing if needed.

BARBARA HEIMANN

MEXICAN CHICKEN SALAD

Our bridge group met at Judy Kaufman's, and she served this salad. We all asked for the recipe!

SALAD:

1 medium head iceberg lettuce, chopped

1 can kidney or black beans, rinsed, and drained

2 cups cooked chicken, chopped

½ cup green pepper, chopped

2 scallions, sliced

OPTIONAL INGREDIENTS:

Avocado, tomato, corn

DRESSING:

⅓ cup cilantro or parsley

3 tablespoons chicken broth

2 tablespoons corn oil

2 tablespoons red wine vinegar

1 tablespoon lime juice

1½ teaspoons sugar

1 clove garlic, minced

¾ teaspoon garlic powder

½ teaspoon salt

Roughly chop all salad ingredients, and mix with dressing.

Place all dressing ingredients in Cuisinart, and mix until totally blended.

❧

R1 SALAD

Gloria had a similar salad at R1 Coffee shop in Boca. She assembled all the ingredients and reproduced it at home. She sent me a picture of it, and I, in turn, made it for my canasta lunch. Deconstructed, it makes a gorgeous presentation. Toss it in front of your guests and sit down to one great lunch!

Serves 4–6

3 cups romaine, thinly sliced horizontally

3 cups baby arugula

¼ pound feta cheese, crumbled

1 cup cooked quinoa

¼ head small red cabbage, very thinly sliced

2 avocados, mashed with a bit of lemon juice

Petite carrots (multi-colored), roasted (available at Trader Joe's), 2–3 carrots per person

Baby tomatoes, halved

DRESSING:

½ tablespoons lemon juice

¼ cup olive oil

1 tablespoon fresh dill, chopped

Salt and pepper to taste

Place carrots on a pan, drizzle some olive oil over, and roast for 15–20 minutes at 400 degrees. This can be done the day before. Cook ½ cup quinoa in 1 cup salted water until light and fluffy. This can even be done in the microwave. Prepare the vegetables. Spread the lettuces on the bottom of a shallow salad bowl. Place the cabbage, mashed avocado, quinoa, tomatoes, and carrots in separate mounds toward the outside rim of the bowl. Place the feta in a mound in the center. Bring the salad to the table along with the dressing and toss just before serving. Adjust the amounts according to the number of guests. Use any dressing that you think would complement this combination.

❧

TOMATO AND POMEGRANATE SALAD

I needed a colorful do-ahead salad for a July 4th party and came across a version by Sam Sifton of an Ottolenghi recipe that I had in his book Plenty More. Don't be ruled by quantities—be generous with the herbs if you like, and use ½ the amount of lemon juice to the olive oil. Pomegranate seeds complement the tomatoes so beautifully—a marriage made in heaven! Following is my interpretation.

6–8 cups baby tomatoes of various colors (baby heirloom tomatoes work well for this)

½ red or yellow pepper, thinly sliced

½ small red onion, thinly sliced and diced

Pomegranate seeds—at least ½ cup

½ cup fresh basil

⅓ cup fresh mint

2 teaspoons za'atar soaked in 1½ tablespoons olive oil to cover

Sea salt

Lemon juice

Olive oil

Feta cheese (optional)

Mix za'atar and oil and set aside.

Cut the tomatoes in half if they are large, if not leave whole; add the pepper and onion and set aside. Do this about an hour before putting together so some of the juices will release from the tomatoes, and then you can drain them before dressing.

When about ready to serve, add pomegranate seeds and gently toss. Tear the herbs, and add. I even added some dried mint to the fresh mint, as I didn't think the balance was right, and it's fine to do so if you don't have enough fresh. Squeeze some lemon juice over, and then add oil and salt. Hold back a bit on the oil, as you will be topping the salad with the za'atar-infused oil. Gently toss. If using feta, sprinkle over the top; then drizzle the za'atar infusion over all.

SAUCES AND DRESSINGS

BUTTERMILK HERB DRESSING

1 cup buttermilk

½ cup low fat mayo

1 tablespoon olive oil

2 tablespoons Italian parsley, chopped

2 tablespoons lemon juice

2 cloves garlic, minced

Salt and pepper to taste—start with ½ teaspoon salt

Blend all together. Prepare the day before planning to use so flavors meld.

DILL VINAIGRETTE

I like to use this vinaigrette over a salad heavily laden with Persian cucumbers, a bit of scallion, and romaine. This salad goes very well with fish as a main course. This vinaigrette is also a good marinade for chicken, just substitute lemon juice for the vinegar.

¼ cup olive oil

¼ cup white wine vinegar

2 teaspoons Dijon mustard

1 teaspoon salt

1 teaspoon pepper, freshly ground

4 tablespoons fresh dill, chopped

Whisk all ingredients except dill until emulsified. Add dill and whisk once more to blend. Enjoy over a salad of your choice.

HORSERADISH SAUCE

We ate at Jane and Ed Kerr's one evening, and they served a delicious fillet with this sauce as an accompaniment.

½ cup heavy (whipping) cream

3 tablespoons horseradish, well drained

1 tablespoon shallot, finely minced

½ teaspoon kosher salt

Pinch of freshly ground black pepper

Beat cream just until it forms soft peaks. Don't over-beat. Whisk in rest of ingredients. Chill until ready to serve. Bring to room temperature. Yields 1 cup—good for one fillet or eight people. I actually doubled the recipe for one fillet. Don't double the salt, however; taste first.

ROMESCO SAUCE

This sauce is good with steak and chicken or as a dip for vegetables.
Use the amounts of paprika and garlic that please your palate.

Serves 4

2 tablespoons sliced almonds, toasted

2 slices whole grain bread, cubed and toasted

1 tablespoon olive oil

1–2 cloves garlic, minced

¼ - ½ teaspoon Spanish smoked paprika

1 tablespoon sherry vinegar

⅛ teaspoon salt

In a food processor, pulse almond and bread until coarsely ground.

Heat olive oil in a small skillet, and add garlic and paprika. Cook for about a minute until the garlic just begins to brown.

Add garlic mixture, vinegar, peppers, and salt to the bread mixture and process until smooth. Adjust seasonings to your taste.

SHALLOT/MUSHROOM GRAVY

2 large shallots

1 tablespoon butter

1 teaspoon dried thyme

12 ounces sliced mushrooms

2 cups chicken broth

Slice shallots thinly, and sauté in butter until wilted and glazed. Add thyme and mushrooms, and continue sautéing until mushrooms release some of their juices and begin to soften. Add broth, and simmer until the liquid is reduced to gravy consistency. Season to taste with salt and pepper. This gravy adds the perfect touch to a roasted turkey breast.

TOMATO JAM

This recipe is from a cooking class at the Ritz. It is so easy to use the currant jelly as a base for all kinds of jams. Just substitute fruit for the tomatoes and be creative!

1 (12 ounce) jar red currant jelly

5 tomatoes, medium large

Core the stem ends of the tomatoes, and cut a small "x" in the opposite ends. Blanch the tomatoes in boiling water for 20 seconds. Using a slotted spoon, remove the tomatoes and plunge into ice water. When the tomatoes cool down, peel away the skins; they should just slip off. Roughly chop the tomatoes, and add them to a small pot along with their juices. Add the jar of jelly and bring to a gentle bubble; continue to cook for 18–22 minutes or until mixture thickens. Cool and store in refrigerator.

*I have made half this recipe using 3 small tomatoes and ½ the jar of jelly.

TOMATO VINAIGRETTE

⅔ cup tomato jam

1 tablespoon cider vinegar

5 tablespoons olive oil

Salt and pepper to taste

Whisk all ingredients together and store in refrigerator.

A delicious salad using this vinaigrette: Romaine. Manchego cheese, and Marcona almonds.

BARBARA HEIMANN

WARM TOMATO DRESSING

This is a very good accompaniment to beef or lamb as well as a light dressing for a lettuce salad.

2 teaspoons olive oil

1 pint cherry tomatoes

3 cloves garlic, minced

⅔ cup dry red wine

¼ cup balsamic vinegar

1 tablespoon sugar

¼ teaspoon salt

1 teaspoon red wine vinegar

Cook tomatoes in oil for 5 minutes. Stir in garlic, red wine, and balsamic vinegar and reduce the liquid by ½, cooking on low for about 5 minutes. Liquid reduces simply by cooking slowly on a low heat. Add remaining 3 ingredients, and cook for 1 minute. Can use right away or refrigerate. Bring to room temperature before serving.

SEAFOOD

PAELLA

COCKTAIL SAUCE

When we were in Youngstown in September 2008, we had a get-together at Anita and Dick Shapiro's house, and Louise Kannensohn brought a platter of shrimp with a wonderful cocktail sauce.

1 cup catsup

1 cup chili sauce

Juice of 1 lemon

¼ cup white horseradish

Mix together all ingredients. Simple enough and good with any seafood.

COCKTAIL SHRIMP

I learned this easy preparation for shrimp with cocktail sauce while living in Arkansas. The beer and pickling spice make it special.

1 pound extra-large shrimp, cleaned, tails on

1 bottle beer

1–2 tablespoons pickling spice

If shrimp are frozen, defrost. Bring beer and pickling spice to a boil, and add shrimp. Return to a boil, and when shrimp are just pink, remove from liquid with a slotted spoon and cool. Serve chilled with cocktail sauce.

1950'S CURRIED SHRIMP

When David and I were first married (at the ripe-old age of 19!), I learned how to make this recipe, and it seemed daunting then—so simple now! When we served it with Matcus wine in the green bottle with the wide gold neckband, we felt so sophisticated. The memory of this dish is still with me.

Serves 4

¼ cup melted butter

¼ cup flour

½ teaspoon salt

Dash paprika

1 teaspoon curry powder

1½ cups milk

3 tablespoons catsup

¼ cup cooking sherry

1½ cups cleaned shrimp

2 cups cooked rice

Blend first 5 ingredients and stir over low heat. Gradually stir in milk. Cook until thick and smooth. Add catsup and sherry and stir. Finally add raw shrimp, and cook until shrimp turn pink and are done.

Serve over rice. Sprinkle with parsley.

CURRIED SHRIMP 21ST CENTURY STYLE

David and I enjoyed this simple dinner on a rare occasion when it was just the two of us!

1 tablespoon olive oil

1 large onion, halved vertically and then thinly sliced

2 carrots, sliced into rounds

2 cloves garlic, minced

2 teaspoons curry powder

1 cup long grain rice

2½ cups water

Salt and pepper

1½ pounds raw shrimp, de-veined

½ cup fresh basil, chiffonade

Sauté chopped vegetables in the olive oil for 6–8 minutes. Add garlic and curry, and continue cooking for 2 minutes. Add rice and 2½ cups water, salt, and pepper. Cover, and simmer for 15 minutes or until rice is almost done. Nestle shrimp into rice, and simmer for 4 more minutes. Remove from heat, and add the fresh basil.

GINGER-APRICOT SHRIMP

Lisa, Robin, and I went to BhaBha, a popular Persian restaurant in Naples, and we ordered this as one of our shared meals. Absolutely delicious! This recipe was published in Bon Appétit, and Michael Mir, the owner, gave me permission to use it in this book. He's such a nice man and sent us some complimentary baklava for dessert, which even though we were so full, we managed to finish as well. It was too good to leave on the plate!

Serves 2-4

12 dried apricot halves

12 pitted prunes

⅔ cup chicken broth, low salt, plus more if needed to add later

2 tablespoons soy sauce

1 tablespoon mango chutney, large pieces chopped

2 teaspoons tamarind concentrate

1 teaspoon sugar

1¼ teaspoons ground cumin

1¼ teaspoons curry powder

1½ teaspoons garlic powder

¼–½ teaspoon cayenne pepper, according to taste

3 tablespoons vegetable oil

½ cup white onion, thinly sliced

2 cloves garlic, minced

1 teaspoon fresh ginger, minced

½ cup matchstick-size carrots

16 large shrimp, uncooked, peeled, de-veined, and butterflied from head to tail (or substitute with 1 pound firm-fleshed white fish, sliced into 2-inch pieces)

1 green onion, chopped

Place apricots and prunes in a small bowl, and add enough boiling water to cover. Let stand 15 minutes to soften. Drain and quarter all fruit.

Meanwhile, mix ⅔ cup broth with soy sauce, mango chutney, tamarind concentrate, and sugar in a small bowl. Whisk cumin, curry powder, garlic powder, and cayenne pepper in another small bowl.

Fruit, broth mixture, and spice blend can be made 2 hours ahead. Let stand separately at room temperature.

Heat oil in large skillet over medium-high heat. Add onion, and sauté until translucent, about 2 minutes. Add garlic and ginger, and sauté 30 seconds. Add apricot, plums, and carrots; sauté until onions begin to brown, about 1 minute. Add shrimp and spice blend, stirring to coat. Cook until shrimp are pink on both sides, but still uncooked in center, about 2 minutes. Add broth mixture; cover, and cook until shrimp are just opaque in center, about 1 minute, adding more broth by spoonfuls if sauce is too thick. Transfer to serving bowl. Sprinkle with green onion, and serve. Steamed rice is a good accompaniment to absorb some of the sauce.

* This can be made just with apricots resulting in a beautiful color.

PAELLA WITH SAFFRON AIOLI

This recipe comes from Ritz Carlton Chef Gary J. Murphy and was appealing to me because of its versatility as a gorgeous dish for a dinner party. I tested the recipe and served it to 7 dinner guests, who are also appreciative eaters. They all gave this "thumbs-up"! The best part is I made most of the recipe the day before and only needed to sauté the seafood right before assembling the dish. Don't be intimidated; just read through, take a deep breath, and proceed. It's easy! Aioli recipe follows.

Serves 10–12

3 tablespoons butter

1 tablespoon olive oil

7 ounces vermicelli noodles, angel hair pasta or fideos

2 cups Arborio rice

4 cups vegetable broth

1 cup clam juice

1 (14½ ounce) can diced tomatoes, strained

10 ounces smoked turkey sausage, sprinkled with smoked paprika, and cut into thin disks, or chorizo, casing removed

1 pinch saffron

2 teaspoons smoked paprika

1 tablespoon garlic powder

2 bay leaves

1 medium onion, small dice

1 red bell pepper, small dice

Salt and pepper to taste

1 cup lobster bisque, added only after rice is done

1½ cups frozen peas, reserve ½ cup for final assembly

½ rotisserie chicken, or 3 cooked breast halves, cut into chunks

2 tablespoons olive oil

2 cloves garlic, minced

1½ pounds raw shrimp, peeled and de-veined

1½ pounds sea scallops or 1 pound mussels, rinsed, beards removed

¼ cup white wine

Garnish: lemon wedges, chopped Italian parsley, aioli

SAFFRON AIOLI:

¼ cup boiling water with 1 pinch saffron added

1 clove garlic, minced

1 cup light mayonnaise

1 lemon, juiced

Salt and pepper to taste

In a large sauté pan, melt butter and olive oil together. Add the noodles, and stir frequently until the noodles are browned. Then add the rice to the noodles and stir. Add the rest of the first set of ingredients through salt and pepper. Cover pan, and cook until rice is cooked through, about 20 minutes. When rice is done, turn off heat, remove bay leaves, and stir in lobster bisque. After 5 minutes the bisque will be absorbed, and then the peas and chicken can be added. After all of this has cooled, remove to another bowl, and refrigerate overnight if you wish.

Preheat oven to 450 degrees.

About two hours before reheating, remove rice from fridge and bring to room temperature. Add remaining ½ cup frozen peas. Put 2 tablespoons olive in a casserole large enough to hold the mixture. Place the oiled casserole dish in the oven, and heat dish and oil until hot, about 5 minutes. At this point, spoon in the rice mixture, return to oven, and heat for about 20 minutes.

While rice is heating, sauté the seafood, each type separately in the garlic oil until just done. If using mussels, cook until mussels open up. Use white wine as needed to keep a bit of liquid in the pan.

Pull rice out of the oven; place seafood over the top of the rice, and garnish with the lemon, parsley, and a dollop of aioli. Serve rest of aioli on the side.

For saffron Aioli: Let saffron water cool. Blend rest of ingredients, and add saffron water a bit at a time until desired consistency. This lasts in the fridge for a week.

❧

SALMON BAKED TWO WAYS

These are such simple preparations, but the end product is as good as can be.

Serves 4–6

Fresh Atlantic salmon, skin off
Paul Prudhomme's salmon seasoning

Preheat oven to 450 degrees. Spray baking pan, and then sprinkle the seasoning over the fish. Bake in center of oven for 10–12 minutes.

Marni made this version for a Rosh Hashanah lunch.

1¾ —2-pound side of salmon—skin off or on, your preference

Salt and pepper

Sumac

Lemon slices

Sprinkle the salmon with salt and pepper and then with the sumac. Thinly slice the lemon, and place the slices on top of the salmon side.

Bake at 425 degrees for 14 minutes.

SALMON PATTIES

1 pound fresh salmon

2 cups tomatoes, small dice

3 eggs

½ cup shallots, finely minced

3 cups bread crumbs, challah if available (1 cup for mixture, 2 cups for breading)

2 tablespoons Dijon mustard

¼ cup chives, chopped

¼ cup parsley, chopped

1 tablespoon dry mustard, sifted

½ cup vegetable oil

Preheat oven to 450 degrees.

Poach salmon in boiling water just to cover for 5 minutes with lid on saucepan.

Remove from water and cool. Place in large bowl and break up into pieces. Add tomato, eggs, shallots, and 1 cup of breadcrumbs, Dijon, chives, and parsley. Season with salt and pepper.

Mix remaining breadcrumbs with sifted dry mustard and place in flat dish.

Shape salmon mixture into 8 patties, and dust on all sides with breadcrumbs.

Pour oil onto baking sheet, and place the baking sheet in 450-degree oven for 5 minutes. Then place the patties on the baking sheet, and cook for 5–7 minutes until golden; turn over and bake for 5 minutes more.

SALMON WITH PENNE AND NORTHERN BEANS

Dinner at Gail and Mel Ufberg's is a treat as they are both such warm hosts, and she is a terrific cook. Needless to say, the food is plentiful and so good the guests usually overeat. But, whatever, there's always tomorrow...

Serves 6–8

1 pound penne

3 cans northern beans, rinsed, and drained

2 teaspoons minced garlic

8–10 sun-dried tomatoes packed in oil, slivered

8 ounces spinach

3 cups low-sodium chicken broth

Salt and pepper to taste

Parmesan cheese

Italian parsley, roughly chopped

Salmon, 6 ounces each per guest

Preheat oven to 450 degrees.

Sauté garlic in olive oil, and add beans and tomatoes. Add spinach, and sauté until wilted. Add ½ cup broth to pan, and simmer. Set aside while penne is cooking to al dente.

When penne is done, drain and then put bean sauce into pot with penne. Add as much parmesan as you like, and then add the rest of the broth to get to a thin sauce consistency.

Bake salmon at 450- degrees for 12 minutes. Place some of the penne in a large soup bowl; then top with the salmon. Garnish with the parsley, and serve extra parmesan at the table.

*If you don't have sun-dried tomatoes, 2 Roma tomatoes seeded and chopped will work just as well.

SALMON WITH ROWS OF VEGGIES

Salmon prepared this way makes a beautiful presentation on a buffet table. This is from Kosher by Design.

1 (3 pound) salmon side

1 zucchini

1 yellow squash

3 Roma tomatoes

¼ cup panko breadcrumbs

2 tablespoons dill

2 tablespoons olive oil

6–8 tablespoons Dijon mustard

Preheat oven to 375 degrees.

Spread Dijon over salmon. Slice unpeeled veggies, very thinly. Place in rows over salmon, alternating with tomatoes. Mix panko, dill, and olive oil. Scatter over top. Bake for 30–35 minutes.

SHRIMP AND CRAB NAPOLEON

This recipe is an adaptation from the Turtle Club in Naples. The Napoleon is my favorite lunch, and I just had to replicate it. The amounts will vary according to taste. I use tuna cans which have both lids removed and have been thoroughly cleaned, as forms for the seafood. You can substitute any cooked, firm white fish for seafood.

SMOKED TOMATO DRESSING:

1 (14 ½ ounce) can diced fire roasted tomatoes, well drained

2 tablespoons white balsamic vinegar

¼ cup vegetable oil

½ teaspoon salt

½ teaspoon sugar

Liquid smoke, a few dashes

SALAD:

1 pound crab meat

1 pound shrimp

Mayonnaise, can be light

Tomato slices

Jicama julienne

Cilantro, or Italian parsley, finely chopped (optional)

BASIL OIL:

2 cups packed basil leaves

½–1 cup olive oil

¼ teaspoon salt

For the smoked tomato dressing: Combine tomatoes, and vinegar in a food processor, and slowly drizzle in oil while continuing to blend. Season with salt, sugar, and a dash or two of liquid smoke. Be sure to shake the bottle of liquid smoke before using.

For the basil oil: Blanch leaves in boiling water for 1 minute. Remove and drain, then pour ice water over until leaves are cold. Press all water out and dry with paper towel. Place ½ cup oil, basil, and salt in blender or processor and puree. Slowly add more oil until thick pouring consistency. This will last about a week in fridge. It's also great drizzled over mashed potatoes, a salad caprese, or as a base for salad dressing.

For the salad: Bind shrimp and crabmeat with just enough mayonnaise hold it together. Place some in the ring of the tuna can, and chill until ready to use. Then, spread some of the vinaigrette in a circle on a plate. Top with a ripe tomato slice. Top that with the well-formed shrimp and crabmeat. Finally, garnish the top and sides with julienne of jicama and fresh cilantro or parsley.

Drizzle a bit of basil oil over top. Serve more dressing on the side.

SNAPPER LIVORNAISE

This recipe comes from Trish Sandstrom. We're cooking class acquaintances, and she likes to cook as much as I do!

Serves 6

2 limes

2 pounds red snapper fillets

Salt

5 tablespoons olive oil

SAUCE:

½ cup chopped onion

3 cloves garlic, crushed

¼ cup olive oil

3 large tomatoes, peeled, seeded, and chopped

1 large bay leaf

½ teaspoon oregano

12 pitted green olives, cut in half

2 tablespoons capers

2 jalapeño peppers, seeded, and cut into strips

½ teaspoon salt

¼ teaspoon freshly ground pepper

1 tablespoon chopped fresh cilantro

1 tablespoon lime juice

Chopped fresh cilantro for garnish

Preheat oven to 325 degrees. Squeeze lime juice over the fish and set aside until ready to cook.

Sauté the onion and garlic in the oil until soft. Stir in remaining ingredients. Season to taste. Cook over medium heat for 10 minutes or until some of liquid has evaporated.

Sprinkle fillets with salt and sear on both sides in oil. Drain and remove to oven-proof casserole or platter. Cover with sauce, and bake for 10–15 minutes. Garnish with chopped cilantro, and serve.

SOUP

CAULIFLOWER SOUP

I had some friends over for a very casual supper, and Sandy Roth brought this soup, which we served in cups as an appetizer.

1 head cauliflower, about 2 pounds

4 tablespoons butter, divided

1 leek, white and light green parts, halved and thinly sliced

1 onion, diced

Salt and pepper

4½ cups water mixed with 1 heaping tablespoon chicken broth mix (I prefer Osem brand)

½ teaspoon sherry vinegar

3 tablespoons chives, finely chopped

Remove outer leaves of cauliflower, and trim stem. Cut heaping 1 cup of ½ inch florets from head of cauliflower and set aside for garnish. Remove core and thinly slice, and then slice remaining cauliflower crosswise into ½ inch slices.

Melt 2 tablespoons butter in large pot over medium-low heat. Add leek, onion, and 1½ teaspoons salt; cook, stirring frequently, until onions are softened, but not browned, about 7 minutes.

Increase heat to medium high; add water and all cauliflower except florets to pot.

While soup simmers, melt remaining 2 tablespoons butter over medium heat in a skillet. Add reserved florets, and cook, stirring frequently until florets are golden brown. Toss florets with vinegar and season with salt to taste.

When cauliflower is soft, process the soup with an immersion blender. If needed, adjust consistency with a bit more water. Season with salt and pepper to taste.

Serve, garnishing individual bowls with browned florets and chives.

CHICKEN SOUP AND POTATO DUMPLINGS (KNEIDLACH)

I reached out to my granddaughter, Marni, an amazing and inventive cook for her chicken soup recipe. She consulted with Jana and Jake, and following is the recipe they developed after years of eating their mother's soup, which has set a high standard. This is exactly as she sent it to me, and you can trust that your soup will be heavenly as well! I have also included my mother Esther Stein's recipe for potato kneidlach—so interesting that this recipe spans 4 generations!

FOR STOCK:

Whole chicken or 4 pounds of bone-in chicken breast and thigh pieces

2–3 onions, skin on, halved

1 pound carrots, washed and unpeeled

6 ribs celery

2 parsnips

6 cloves garlic

Small piece of pumpkin or squash

1 large bunch dill

1 bunch parsley

Salt and pepper

FOR SOUP:

2 onions, quartered

4 carrots, roughly chopped

4 ribs celery, roughly chopped

2 parsnip, roughly chopped

2 zucchini, roughly chopped

1 butternut squash, cubed (optional)

Dill, chopped

Parsley, chopped

Salt and pepper to taste

Make stock: Place all stock ingredients in a very large pot and cover with water. Bring to a boil over high heat. Reduce to a simmer and skim off any foam. Cover and allow to simmer for 2 to 3 hours.

Once stock is done, remove chicken into a bowl and strain the stock. Discard strained veggies and place stock aside. Season with salt and pepper to taste. Once chicken is cool, shred into small chunks and set aside. At this point, you may either freeze the stock and finish the soup later or reserve the stock to continue making the soup.

Make soup: Add soup vegetables except for zucchini and squash (if using) into a large pot with a bit of oil, and sauté until just soft. Pour pre-made stock over vegetables and bring back to a boil. Add chicken and remaining vegetables. Simmer for 5–10 minutes, until zucchini is just soft. Adjust seasoning to taste, and garnish with dill and parsley. Serve with matzo balls and/or kreplach.

POTATO KNEIDLACH

If you want to go a delicious step further than matzo balls, try these. Stuffed with some caramelized onions or gribenes, and served in home-made chicken soup with chunks of chicken and vegetables, this is one complete sublime meal! Definitely this brings back memories of my mother hand-grating the potatoes and stuffing them with just a tiny bit of gribenes that she had made from the small pieces of chicken skin and onions rendered until they were crispy.

6 large potatoes, grated and pressed through a towel

1 egg

1 grated onion

1 cup flour, plus more if needed

2 teaspoons baking powder

Salt and pepper to taste

Pot of salted water brought to a boil

Combine the prepared potatoes, egg, and onion. Mix the baking powder into the flour, and add this mixture into the potatoes. The mixture should be firm enough to form into a ball. If not, add more flour. Season with salt and pepper. Form into golf ball size and stuff with onions or gribenes if you like. Place in boiling salted water; then turn heat down to simmer for 1 hour. Remove with slotted spoon and place in soup bowl.

CREAM OF CUCUMBER SOUP

David's cousin Betty Etkind, who looks just like Elizabeth Taylor and just as glamorous, is a professional chef, and has held top catering positions both in her native Johannesburg and in Sydney, Australia, where she moved to join her children. On one visit, she shared this with me. Think vichyssoise with a twist, and only 72 calories per serving!

Serves 10

1 tablespoon butter

1 onion, finely chopped

8 ounces golden potatoes, diced fine

1 quart chicken or vegetable broth

½ to ¾ cup fresh dill, chopped and loosely packed

1½ teaspoons white wine vinegar

1 tablespoon mustard powder

Salt and pepper to taste

1½ pounds cucumbers, seeded and grated

Cream or evaporated milk to lighten soup

Chopped dill and grated cucumber for garnish

Melt butter in large pot, and sauté onions until transparent but not brown. Add potatoes, broth, dill, vinegar, mustard, salt, and pepper, and cook until vegetables are soft. Cool until able to puree. Then add cucumber, and cook for 10 more minutes. Chill. When ready to serve, thin down with cream. Garnish with cucumber and dill.

CURRIED SQUASH AND RED LENTIL SOUP

Kathy Tamarkin, an excellent cook, was so pleased with this recipe, and as I'm always looking for good vegetarian meals, I was delighted to know about this soup. This is best made a day before planning to serve.

3 tablespoons vegetable oil

2 tablespoons unsalted butter

1½ pound butternut squash, peeled, and cut into 1/2-inch pieces

1 large onion, chopped

1 carrot, chopped

1 celery rib, chopped

2 cloves garlic, minced

2 tablespoons minced, peeled ginger

1 tablespoon curry powder (preferably Madras)

¼ teaspoon pepper, freshly ground

1 cup red lentils, picked over and rinsed

2 quarts water or 1 quart veggie stock/1 quart water

1 teaspoon fresh lemon or lime juice, or to taste

Accompaniment: cooked basmati rice (optional)

Heat oil with butter in a large heavy pot over medium heat until foam subsides; then cook squash, onion, carrot, celery, garlic, ginger, and 1 teaspoon salt, stirring occasionally, until vegetables are softened and beginning to brown, 15–20 minutes.

Stir in curry powder and ¼ teaspoon pepper, and cook, stirring frequently, 2 minutes.

Add lentils and water, and simmer, covered, until lentils are tender, 25–40 minutes. Stir in lemon juice and season with salt and pepper. Serve as is or for a main dish meal; serve over some cooked basmati rice.

HEARTY VEGETABLE SOUP

Gloria was hungry for some vegetable soup, so I went to the grocery store and bought some items and came up with this. Sometimes I add a pinch of sugar to the canned diced tomatoes.

2 (32 ounces each) boxes Imagine No Chicken broth or any vegetable broth

1 can (14 ounces) diced tomatoes

2 leeks, white part only, sliced

1 onion, coarsely diced

Celery with leaves 3 stalks, sliced

2–3 carrots, chunked

12 ounces mushrooms, sliced

1 clove garlic, minced

1 (9 ounce) bag power girl greens—spinach, Swiss chard, kale

1 large sweet potato, peeled and chunked

½ butternut squash cubed or calabash squash

1-2 zucchini or yellow squash, sliced

Dill, handful

Parsley, handful

Ginger (optional)

2 tablespoons Osem chicken-style consommé dissolved in 1 cup water

---

Sauté onions, leeks, celery, carrots, mushrooms, and garlic. Add sweet potato, squash, and zucchini.

Add broth, tomatoes, greens, and herbs, and simmer until all vegetables are soft.

Add the dissolved Osem broth. Taste for seasoning with salt and pepper. Turn heat off, and let cool down a bit. Then use an immersion blender, and blend until some soup is slightly chunky and other pieces are left intact.

LENTIL SOUP

Myra Benedict served this soup to five-star reviews. She got the recipe from her daughter, Lesley, who lives in Tel Aviv.

2 large sweet onions, chopped

4 stalks celery, diced

4 carrots, diced

3 medium tomatoes, chopped, or 2 (14½ ounce) cans diced tomatoes, drained, saving juice

2 tablespoons olive oil

1 teaspoon ground ginger (or 1 tablespoon from tube)

1 teaspoon ground curry to taste

½ teaspoon ground cumin

½ teaspoon ground turmeric

1 tablespoon sugar

6 cups broth (vegetable, chicken, or beef) plus 1½–2 cups more if needed to thin soup

2 tablespoons tomato paste

6–8 tablespoons red lentils

6–8 tablespoons brown or green lentils

3 tablespoons chopped fresh cilantro or parsley, plus extra for sprinkling

1½ teaspoons freshly ground black pepper and kosher salt, to taste

6 cloves garlic, coarsely chopped

1 tablespoon flour

1 (6 ounce) package spinach leaves (optional)

½ teaspoon cinnamon, or to taste

2 eggs, lightly beaten

2 tablespoons lemon juice

Sauté the onions in olive oil until translucent and then celery and carrots. Add tomatoes, and cook until onions are lightly browned. Sprinkle in ginger, curry, cumin, turmeric, and sugar, cooking another moment or two to bring out the flavors of the spices.

Stir in broth, liquid from canned tomatoes, tomato paste, lentils, cilantro, black pepper, salt, and garlic. Bring to a boil; then reduce the heat, and simmer uncovered until the lentils are just tender, about 40 minutes. Add some hot liquid to the flour, and blend well. Stir in the flour mixture to the soup.

Myra added 1½ cups more broth at this point, since the soup had cooked down a fair amount. If using spinach, add to soup.

Blend in the cinnamon. Beat the eggs and lemon juice. Drizzle into soup, letting the egg string into tiny delicate strands.

Serve each bowlful with a scattering of cilantro and wedge of lemon or lime for each person to squeeze in.

MUSHROOM SOUP, FRESH!

Myra Benedict made this for a bridge lunch, and we happily managed to polish it off!

6 cups

1 pound fresh mushrooms—any variety or a combination

6 tablespoons butter or margarine

2 cups onions, chopped

1 tablespoon brown sugar

¼ cup flour

1 cup water

1¾ cups chicken broth

¼ cup dry vermouth or dry sherry

¼ teaspoon dried thyme, crushed in fingers

1 teaspoon salt

¼ teaspoon black pepper, coarsely ground

Slice ⅓ of mushrooms, and finely dice the rest. Set aside.

Melt butter in pot, and add onion and brown sugar. Cook over medium heat, stirring constantly, about 15 minutes until onions are caramel colored. Add all the mushrooms, and sauté 5 minutes. Then add flour, stirring until smooth, and cook about one more minute while stirring. Gradually add water, broth, and vermouth or sherry. Cook over medium heat until slightly thickened. Reduce heat; add thyme and seasonings, and simmer for 10 minutes.

POTATO SOUP

My high-school buddy, Dr. Jack Wassil, brought me this recipe the last time we met for coffee in Sharon, PA. It's from the Shenango Inn, which was a beautiful landmark hotel for years. The chef, Helen Monoc, devised this Czechoslovakian recipe, which, through a congressional bill, became the official daily soup in Capitol Hill restaurants.

Serves 8

4 medium potatoes cut into small cubes

1 cup celery, chopped

½ cup onions, chopped

1 carrot, diced

2 teaspoons salt

2 tablespoons butter

1 quart milk, scalded, can use 2 %, but not skim

2 tablespoons parsley, chopped

1 tablespoon pimento, chopped

DUMPLINGS:

2 eggs

2 tablespoons cold water

Pinch salt

Flour, just enough to make a soft dough

Place the potatoes, celery, onions, and carrot in a saucepan. Add water with the 2 teaspoons salt to cover the vegetables, and cook until tender. Add 2 tablespoons butter. To this add the scalded milk, parsley, and pimento. Add more salt and pepper to taste.

While soup is simmering, make the dumplings. Stir together the eggs, water, and salt, and add just enough flour to make soft dough. Pinch off small pieces, and add to the soup.

More milk may be added if soup is too thick.

SOUTHWESTERN CORN AND SWEET POTATO SOUP

Our bridge group has lunch together, and when we were playing at Lynni Mendelson's, she served this wonderful soup—recipe from her daughter, Robin Kourakis, who normally doubles the recipe.

1 cup onion, finely chopped

2 cloves garlic, minced

1 small chili, seeded and minced

¼ teaspoon salt

3 cups vegetable stock

2 teaspoons cumin, ground

1 medium sweet potato, chunked—about 2 cups

1 red pepper, finely chopped

3 cups corn, fresh or frozen

Salt and pepper to taste

Garnish: lime wedges, cilantro

Simmer onion, garlic, chili, and salt in 1 cup broth for about 10 minutes. In small bowl, make paste with cumin and 1 tablespoon of stock and stir into pot.

Add sweet potatoes and rest of stock, and simmer until potatoes are soft. Then add red pepper and corn, and simmer until these veggies are tender.

Puree ½ the soup in blender and return to pot, season to taste. When serving can shred some cilantro on top of soup in bowl and offer lime wedges.

WEDDING SOUP

For many years, I had thought wedding soup was a Youngstown creation, but lately I have seen it on the menu in many Italian restaurants. However, you need not go out to dinner to experience this delicious and filling soup. Some crusty bread and a salad would complete a supper at home.

MEATBALLS:

1 pound ground chicken

½ cup breadcrumbs

¼ cup Parmesan, grated

⅛ cup parsley, finely chopped

1 egg

1/3 small onion, grated

¼ teaspoon garlic powder

1 teaspoon salt

½ teaspoon pepper

SOUP:

2 quarts chicken broth

1 stalk celery and leaves, chopped

4 (10 ounce) packages chopped spinach, well drained

2 chicken breasts, skinned, bone-in

2 chicken thighs, skinned, bone-in

1 egg

2 tablespoons Parmesan, grated

Mix all ingredients for meatballs; set aside. Simmer broth and celery. Add chicken parts, and cook at a low boil until almost done; then remove from soup, cool, and de-bone. Form meatball mixture into ¾- inch balls and drop into the simmering soup. Simmer for 10 minutes, and then add strained spinach. When meatballs are firm, return chicken to the soup. Simmer 5 more minutes. At this point, the soup can be frozen, refrigerated, or set aside until ready to serve. Just before serving, scramble the egg with a fork, and let the egg just drizzle into the soup off the tines of the fork. The egg will cook rapidly. Finally, add the Parmesan and love every spoonful!

WEST AFRICAN PEANUT SOUP

Lisa gave me this recipe when I asked her for one of her favorites. She told me this was her Mom's, so I trialed it when Stephanie was here, and I liked it. I love peanut butter on apples so tried some apples grated as a garnish for the bowl of soup!

2 cups chopped onion

2 teaspoons vegetable oil

2 teaspoons olive oil

½ teaspoon cayenne

1–2 teaspoons grated fresh ginger

1 cup chopped carrots

2 cups chopped sweet potato

4 cups vegetable stock (Imagine Vegetarian no-Chicken Broth)

1 can chopped tomatoes in juice

1 cup smooth peanut butter (buy just with peanuts as the ingredient)

1 tablespoon sugar

Salt to taste

Apple, grated for garnish (optional)

Sauté the onions in oil till translucent. Stir in the cayenne and fresh ginger. Add the carrots, and sauté a couple of more minutes. Add the potatoes and stock. Bring to boil, and then simmer for 15 minutes, until vegetables are tender. Puree the soup with the can of tomatoes and juice in a blender, or preferably, use an immersion blender. Return the puree to pot and stir in the peanut butter until smooth. Reheat very gently. Add a little sugar and/or salt as needed. If too thick, can add a little more stock, water, or tomato juice. When serving, top with about a tablespoon of grated apple, if you like.

*Soup cannot be hot when using a blender. Cool first; then just fill blender half full to blend.

VEGETABLES

FRENCH DINNER CENTERPIECE

BRUSSELS SPROUTS WITH GRAPES AND WALNUTS

I received a catalog from Whole Foods advertising their Thanksgiving foods. This recipe was included as a "side that steals the spotlight." I tried the recipe, and it was too easy and good not to share.

4 cups Brussels sprouts, halved

2 cups red seedless grapes

½ cup walnuts, roughly chopped

2 tablespoons olive oil

2 tablespoons thyme, fresh preferred, but can use dried, only use less

Sea salt and freshly ground pepper to taste

2–3 tablespoons balsamic vinegar or balsamic glaze

Preheat oven to 400 degrees.

Trim Brussels sprouts and halve. Place sprouts, grapes, and walnuts in a bowl and toss with the olive oil, thyme, salt, and pepper. Then place on a rimmed baking sheet. I always use parchment paper on the sheet for easy cleanup. Bake for 20–25 minutes, turning halfway through. Sprouts and nuts should look toasted and the grapes should plump up. When just out of the oven, drizzle the balsamic vinegar and toss to coat. Transfer to serving dish and sprinkle with a little additional sea salt, and tear some thyme leaves over top.

CAULIFLOWER COUSCOUS

Serves 6–8

1 head cauliflower

3 tablespoons sesame seeds, toasted

2 teaspoons smoked paprika

Zest of 2 lemons

Juice of 1 lemon, reserving juice of second lemon for adjusting taste when recipe completed

2 cloves garlic, minced

½ cup olive oil

Salt and pepper to taste

Mint, handful, leaves torn

Chives, handful, diced

Bring pot of salted water to boil, and add cauliflower florets; boil just a few minutes until soft, yet resistant to tip of knife. Drain, and when cool and dry, pulse in food processor until cauliflower resembles couscous.

Whisk all ingredients together, except for juice from one lemon. Fold in the cauliflower and adjust seasonings, adding more juice, oil, or salt and pepper to taste.

When ready to serve, toss in herbs.

*Cauliflower couscous can be purchased at some stores, ready to be boiled and prepared. If using the couscous this way, just quickly immerse the couscous in the boiling water.

BARBARA HEIMANN

CAULIFLOWER-LEEK KUGEL WITH ALMOND-HERB CRUST

Paula Domsky gave me this recipe. This is a wonderful Passover side dish. This can be prepared eight hours ahead; cover and chill before bringing to room temperature and baking.

Serves 8

8 cups cauliflower florets (from 2 medium heads of cauliflower)

6 tablespoons olive oil, divided

4 cups coarsely chopped leeks (white and pale green parts, from 3 large)

6 tablespoons unsalted matzo meal or panko crumbs

3 large eggs

½ cup chopped fresh parsley, 1 tablespoon set aside

½ cup chopped fresh dill, 1 tablespoon set aside

1½ teaspoons salt

½ teaspoon coarsely ground black pepper

⅓ cup almonds, toasted, chopped

Cook cauliflower in large pot of boiling salted water until tender, about 10 minutes. Drain; transfer to large bowl and mash coarsely with potato masher.

Heat 3 tablespoons oil in heavy large skillet over medium-high heat. Add leeks, and sauté until tender and just beginning to color, about 5 minutes. Add leek mixture to cauliflower. Mix in matzo meal. Beat eggs, 1 tablespoon parsley, 1 tablespoon dill, and then the salt and pepper in small bowl to blend; stir into cauliflower mixture. Preheat oven to 350 degrees.

Brush 11x7 inch baking dish with 1 tablespoon oil. Spread cauliflower mixture evenly in prepared dish. Mix almonds, remaining parsley and dill, and 2 tablespoons oil in medium bowl to blend. Sprinkle evenly over kugel. Bake kugel uncovered until set in center and beginning to brown on top, about 35 minutes. Let stand 10 minutes before serving.

GREEN BEANS WITH CRISPY SHALLOTS

½ cup vegetable oil

4–5 shallots, thinly sliced into rings

2 tablespoons butter or margarine

2 tablespoons olive oil

2 pounds fresh green beans

Salt and pepper to taste

In a medium frying pan, heat the ½ cup oil, and fry the shallots 5–7 minutes until crispy. Be patient, and watch them while stirring to get each piece crispy. Remove to paper towels with a slotted spoon, and drain. Discard the oil. These can be done a day ahead.

Heat the butter and oil together; add the green beans, and sauté about 5 minutes until beans are bright green. Season, and remove from heat. Top with the crispy shallots.

❧

GREEN BEANS, ROASTED

Serves 4

1 pound green beans

1 tablespoon olive oil

½ teaspoon salt

Pepper, freshly ground

Preheat oven to 450 degrees. Line a rimmed baking pan with aluminum foil. Place beans in pan and drizzle oil over; season with salt and pepper. With hands, distribute the oil through beans, and arrange beans in an even layer. Roast in middle position in oven for 10 minutes.

Redistribute beans and roast 10 minutes longer until beans show signs of browning and begin to shrivel.

Variations:

1. Add ½ medium red onion — sliced, to step 1 and roast with beans.

2. Or, mix 1 tablespoon balsamic vinegar, 1 teaspoon honey, ½ teaspoon dried thyme, and 2 medium thinly sliced garlic cloves. Then add this mixture after redistributing for the last 10 minutes. When done, sprinkle 1/3 cup toasted walnuts over.

3. Or, make a mixture of 1 tablespoon minced garlic, 1 teaspoon minced ginger, 2 teaspoons honey, ½ teaspoon sesame oil, and ¼ teaspoon red pepper flakes. Add this after redistributing for last 10 minutes of roasting.

MASHED POTATOES

What? A recipe for something we all make without thinking? Well, this is a twist, and one I picked up at my Ritz cooking class. The secret is olive oil.

Serves 4

2 pounds Yukon gold potatoes, peeled, and cut into medium chunks

2 lemon, juiced and zested

4–6 tablespoons extra virgin olive oil

6 tablespoons chives, chopped

Salt and pepper to taste

Place potatoes in pot and cover with salted water. Bring the potatoes to a boil and then turn heat to medium. Cook for about 15 minutes until they are fork tender.

Strain the potatoes in a colander set over a bowl. Save the liquid in the bowl.

Mash the potatoes and then mix with the lemon juice, zest, olive oil, chives, and salt and pepper to taste. Use some of the reserved liquid from cooking the potatoes to thin to your preferred consistency.

PARTY POTATOES

This recipe comes from Brenda, who is a terrific cook, but sometimes when she gives me recipes, they lack specific amounts. This works for someone as experienced as she, but can pose a problem for the new cook. That said, you can't go wrong with this—just try it!

Serves 8–10

*Adjust amounts for number of people.

3 pounds new potatoes, scrubbed but not peeled

3 Vidalias, at least, cut into thick slices

½ cup Dijon mustard

1/3 cup brown sugar

3 cloves garlic, minced

1 tablespoon paprika

Salt to taste

Canola oil

Preheat oven to 350 degrees. Cut potatoes into bite-size pieces. Mix the rest of the ingredients, but not the oil. Then slowly add the oil until you have made a paste. Toss all the potatoes, onions, and the mustard paste together, coating everything well. On a parchment-lined pan, lay the potatoes out as thinly as possible. Bake for 1½ hours, mixing every half hour, making sure all is browned well.

*To prepare the day before, cook for 1 hour and then finish before ready to serve. Or, prepare in morning and leave on counter until ready to bake.

POTATO GRATIN

I found this recipe on Epicurious, and since I was making a French-themed dinner party, it was an outstanding addition to the meal. It's absolutely delicious, easy, and très bon!

Serves 8

3 pounds russet potatoes, peeled and sliced into 1/8-inch rounds

1½ cups crème fraiche

1½ cups Gruyère, grated (about 6 ounces)

2 tablespoons Italian parsley, finely chopped (optional)

Preheat oven to 400 degrees.

Generously butter a 9×13 inch or a 10–12-inch round baking dish. Arrange half of potatoes in pan, overlapping slightly. Salt and pepper potatoes. Spread ½ crème fraiche over, and then sprinkle ½ of Gruyère over first layer. And then repeat process. Arrange remaining potatoes, salt and pepper, and crème fraiche, and then top with Gruyère. Bake gratin uncovered for 30 minutes; then reduce oven temperature to 350 degrees, and continue baking until potatoes are tender and top is golden brown, about another 30 minutes. When done, remove from oven, and let stand 10 minutes before serving. If using parsley, sprinkle over the top of the gratin.

*For a dinner party, I like to get as much done ahead of time as possible. The day before the party, prepare the gratin, baking only for the first 30 minutes. Cool and refrigerate. Bring it to room temperature and finish baking in time for dinner.

**A large russet potato is close to 1 pound, so figure on 3–4 potatoes. I made this in a small pan using 1 potato, ½ cup crème fraiche, and ½ cup Gruyère.

SPAGHETTI SQUASH WITH ITALIAN TOMATO/VEGETABLE SAUCE

I'm cleaning out my pantry, as I'm getting ready to move back into my condo, which has been under renovation. I had all these ingredients other than the squash, and they turned the ordinary into something quite appetizing.

3 pounds spaghetti squash

1 tablespoon olive oil

1 large Vidalia onion, diced

3 carrots, diced

6 mini peppers, sliced into thin rings, or 1 red pepper

1 (28 ounce) can diced tomatoes with Italian herbs

Parmesan cheese, grated

Preheat oven to 400 degrees.

Bake squash in oven for 45 minutes or until the outer shell becomes slightly soft. Remove from oven and cool. Cut squash in half lengthwise and remove all the seeds. Set aside. While squash is baking, sauté onion in olive oil for 5 minutes on medium-low heat, and then add carrots and peppers. Sauté until all vegetables are done, about 15 minutes on low heat. Season vegetables with salt and pepper. Add can of tomatoes, and mix through. Using a fork, scrape the pulp out of the spaghetti squash shell right into the vegetable mixture. Separate the pulp into strands, and mix through. At this point, just enjoy with a sprinkling of Parmesan on top.

*In a 350-degree oven, this can also be baked with some shredded mozzarella on top until the cheese is melted and the squash is heated through.

BARBARA HEIMANN

SQUASH CHILI

Stephanie and Lisa were coming for a visit, and when I inquired where I should make some reservations for dinner, the answer was "we just want to hang with you and eat your cooking." So to get ahead of the game, I made this chili, which does well in the freezer. One less thing to do last minute!

2 cans red kidney beans

2 tablespoons olive oil

1 onion, chopped

1 red pepper, chopped

2 jalapeños, chopped

3 cloves garlic, minced

1 tablespoon chili powder

1 tablespoon kosher salt

½ teaspoon smoked paprika

2 pounds butternut squash, chopped into ½ inch pieces

2 cups fresh corn kernels, from 3 ears

1 (14½ ounce) can diced tomatoes

4 cups veggie broth

Mash ½ cup of kidney beans and set aside with rest of beans. Sauté onions, garlic, jalapeños, and red bell pepper for 5 minutes. Stir in chili powder, salt, cumin, and paprika. Stir 1 minute. Stir in rest of ingredients, and cook until squash is tender.

SQUASH STUFFED WITH AUTUMN VEGETABLES

The Autumnal Equinox brings a burst of cooking energy to Stephanie. I just got a phone call from her as she was heading home from the grocery store laden with the ingredients for this recipe. You're on your own with amounts!

Acorn or butternut squash, halved lengthwise

Onion

Mushrooms

Poblano pepper

Red pepper

Carrots

Corn

Cheddar cheese, finely diced

Salt

Cayenne pepper

Preheat oven to 375 degrees.

Bake squash until soft enough to scoop out flesh and still have shells intact. Sauté onions until soft; add mushrooms, peppers, carrots, and corn. Cook until slightly underdone. Add scooped-out squash and cheddar. Season with salt and cayenne. The mixture can either be put back into the squash shells or baked in a casserole, which has been heated with 2 tablespoons oil for 5 minutes. Then bake casserole for 30 minutes until nicely browned.

TOMATO, CHARD, AND GRUYÈRE CASSEROLE

I saw the recipe for this casserole in Food and Wine magazine and decided to try it when tomatoes were at their most flavorful. I found their recipe a bit too bready, so I made it with thinly sliced bread. This list of ingredients will make a very large casserole—enough to feed 12 at least, but I cut it in half and used a 2-quart casserole.

5½ pounds Swiss chard, stemmed

¼ cup olive oil

2 large onions, thinly sliced

1 tablespoon chopped thyme

1 cup dry white wine

Salt and freshly ground pepper

3 cups chicken broth (I use veggie broth)

1 loaf (1 pound) day-old peasant bread sliced ⅓-inch thick

3 pounds beefsteak tomatoes, sliced ½-inch thick

9 ounces (3 cups) Gruyère cheese, shredded

3 tablespoons unsalted butter, melted

Preheat oven to 400 degrees.

Cook chard for 2 minutes in large pot of boiling water and then drain. When leaves are cool enough, squeeze out all the water; then coarsely chop the chard.

In the same pot, sauté the onions and thyme in the olive oil on medium-low heat for 12 minutes. Add the chard and wine, and cook until wine is reduced to ¼ cup.

Butter a 10 x 15- inch baking dish. Line the bottom with ⅓ of the bread, cutting the bread to fit the pan. Top with half the tomato slices, and season with salt and pepper. Spread ½ the chard on top and then ½ the Gruyère. Repeat procedure once more, and place last ⅓ of bread slices on top. Pour broth over all, and with a spatula, press contents down into the casserole.

Brush the melted butter over the bread. Cover with aluminum foil. Bake in top ⅓ of oven for 1 hour; then remove foil, and bake uncovered for 10 minutes. Let the casserole rest for 10–15 minutes before serving.

TWICE-BAKED POTATOES WITH CARAMELIZED SHALLOTS

Ten of us longtime Youngstown friends got together on New Year's Eve of 2013. We all saw the film Les Miserables and then came back to my condo for a delicious meal. Everyone pitched in, and Myra Benedict brought this potato preparation. However, she didn't follow the recipe exactly, and we each happily ended up eating one whole stuffed potato. "Stuffed" being the operative word here!

These small potato cups (each one is half a russet potato) are a great choice if you're short on oven space. The potatoes can be baked and stuffed one day ahead and chilled; then warmed in the oven for 20 minutes while the meat rests before carving.

Makes 8 servings

4 each (12 ounce) russet potatoes, scrubbed

Vegetable oil

1 cup coarsely grated Havarti cheese (about 4 ounces)

½ cup sour cream

½ cup whole milk

¼ teaspoon cayenne pepper

3 tablespoons butter

1 1/2 cups thinly sliced shallots (about 8 ounces)

1 tablespoon chopped fresh Italian parsley

Preheat oven to 400 degrees.

Pierce potatoes in several places with fork and then brush lightly with oil. Place potatoes directly on oven rack, and bake until tender when pierced with fork, about 55 minutes. Cool potatoes slightly.

Cut off thin slice from both short ends of each potato, and discard. Cut each potato crosswise in half; stand each half on its small flat end. Using teaspoon, scoop out cooked potato pulp from each half, leaving a 1/3-inch thick shell and forming potato cup. Place potato cups in 9 × 13- inch baking dish. Place potato pulp in medium bowl; add cheese, sour cream, milk, and cayenne. Using potato masher or fork, mash until well blended and almost smooth. Season to taste with salt and pepper. Mound mashed potato mixture in potato cups.

Melt butter in heavy medium skillet over medium heat. Add shallots, and sauté until tender and deep brown, about 12 minutes. Top potato cups with shallots (Can be made 1 day ahead. Cover and chill).

Preheat oven to 350 degrees.

Bake potato cups until heated through, about 20 minutes. Sprinkle with parsley, and serve.

AND FINALLY... GOING TO THE DOGS!